Practical Landlording: How to own and manage investment properties while keeping your sanity intact

By Caryl Rosenthal

For Jerry, who taught me everything I know and for Andy, who taught me everything else.

Table of Contents

Introduction 3

Chapter 1: What Kind of Income Property Do I Want? 5

Chapter 2: What is a Landlord? 10

Chapter 3: Business is Business – Keeping the Tenant at Arm's Length 11

Chapter 4: A Contract is a Contract is a Contract (sort of) . 17

Chapter 5: Familiarity Breeds Contempt, or: Melting the Barriers Between Us and Them 23

Chapter 6: Time and Aggravation Savers, or: You Knew You'd Think of It Eventually! 30

Chapter 7: Roaches and Other Bugs, or: The High Cost of Tuition in the School of Hard Knocks 35

Chapter 8: Hunting for Tenants and Keeping Them Happy 41

Chapter 9: Know Thy Rules 48

Chapter 10: The Next Level, or: Where do I go from here? 53

Introduction

I take full responsibility for being the laziest person ever plopped on the face of the earth. I hate to move from here to there unless there is no other choice; I'd rather put off until tomorrow that which I could otherwise do today; I'll opt for the elevator over the stairs every time.

You might think that my love of creature comforts would clash with my preferred physical position, which is prone. I like to live well. I refuse to drive a car that is beneath my worth. I believe that matched luggage should come from Louis Vuitton. I agree with Marilyn, that diamonds are a girl's best friend, and all that glitters is gold, especially if I am wearing it around my neck or on my fingers.

I don't come from particularly lazy stock. My grandfather's philosophy was that one has plenty of time to sleep after one is dead. Contrary to my upbringing, then, my lifestyle is carefully planned and nurtured. My husband would agree with my grandfather and call it a character flaw; you can decide for yourself.

I'm here to confirm the adage that opposites attract. It therefore stands to reason that if I'm the quintessential sloth, that my marital counterpart is a workaholic whose mission is to be as busy as I am not.

I once asked my husband if he considered himself to be lazy. He straightened with righteous indignation, harrumphed or a minute and replied, "I don't have a lazy bone in my body. Have you ever known me to be lazy?"

Of course, at the time of this conversation, he was attempting to toss a rope around the neck of a teasingly frisky half-Holstein calf, which, unrestrained, was running just out of reach, and which was in the process of wearing down my stocky life's mate while I stood in the shade, watching. "You want to help out here?" he demanded, once again coiling the still-empty rope into his left hand.

I stood up, walked behind the calf, and herding it into the corner where the chain-link fence sections met, headed the now-cooperative calf into the "L" this created. Once trapped, it stood quietly while I slipped the noose around its neck.

I handed my True Love the unoccupied end of the rope. "That's the problem," I responded. "If you were as lazy as I am, you'd figure out how not to work so hard."

So I learned not to apologize for shortcuts which promote my desire to avoid sweat. I continue to go with the flow, directing it with minimal effort to where I want it to end up, while my Prince continues as a workaholic, and more and more as the years go by, the rocks in his head seem to fit the holes in mine.

What does any of this have to do with getting into the fray with tenants, property taxes, and leaky pipes? It's a Great American Success Story, that's what!

Well, my life's partner, a doctor of pharmacy by chosen profession, soon tired of the ranch and chasing calves around while I stood and watched, decided that he would happier in the city, any city, and so he jumped at the first opportunity to turn in his barbed wire fence repair tool for a built-in sprinkler system, complete with timer, and a Farmall tractor's brush-hog for a gas-powered lawnmower. After selling the herd, away we went to Abilene, Texas, an isolated community of approximately 166,000 souls.

Abilene lies some 175 miles west of Fort Worth, 175 miles east of Midland/Odessa, and going north-to-south, there is nothing but infinity in either direction.

There is an airport, but no jet service in or out; there is train service, but freight only; no shuttle bus service to the closest jet-enhanced airports at Dallas/Ft. Worth or Midland/Odessa, or to Lubbock International Airport, some 220 miles to the west-northwest. Once, five, count 'em, five jets headed for DFW were diverted to Abilene. It made the evening news. What does that tell you?

Because of Abilene's distance from any other civilized collection of communities, I was able to put together an entire concept of acquiring, managing, and finally, selling rental income property which I believe I would not have been available to me in a location which did not have as a major identifying feature the intentional isolation of the community. In essence, Abilene was an inherent laboratory for effective development and use of theories and practice, which I want to share with you here

In addition, the cost and manner of acquisition was unique in that the real estate market was as isolated and free from influence of contemporary methods of valuation and financing as It remains free from outside influences in just about every other aspect of American life there is.

But I am getting ahead of myself here. Both my husband and I were born and raised in Los Angeles, a world away from Abilene, Texas. Neither of us ever dreamed that we would ever leave California, much less end up in the middle of a dry, dusty West Texas town. Both of us were educated in L.A., he in pharmacy at the University of Southern California and I, once our children were in school, from California State University at Northridge. In those days, I was just a woman taking up space, as my contemporaries used to constantly remind me, and especially when I said I wanted to go to law school.

I began law school, but for a variety of reasons, I found that I really enjoyed business, especially the Southern California real estate boom of the 1980s. With the encouragement of two friends who had become real estate brokers, I followed through and earned my own broker's license. I finally finished law school 25 years later, but that's another story.

While in training for my broker's license, I learned how to negotiate, how to avoid ambiguities, how to finance, and how to put together a deal which will stick, whether it is between a seller and buyer, buyer and seller, or landlord and tenant, and any other combination thereof.

Chapter 1: What Kind of Income Property Do I Want?

Obviously, there is more financial security when the risk is spread out over more than a single rental unit at one location. However many units you can feel you can handle at one time, it is best to purchase property which does not require on-site management. There are several reasons for this.

Managing the property yourself means having fewer units at one location. I always prefer two to six units at any one location, although eight might be feasible. More units than that invites trouble without on-site management. Then it becomes a question of which is worse: a permanent management presence with the attendant loss of control of your investment, or biting more than one person can comfortably chew.

When you opt for on-site management, there are some factors to consider which should influence your decision. First, in a ten- or 12-unit building, the cost of giving up all or part of the income from a single unit may not be cost effective. You would have to offer a free apartment, or at least reduced rent, to the person managing the building. By comparison, apartment complexes hire professional management firms or hire their own personnel who do not necessarily live on-site.

With a limited number of units, another management problem is that there are going to be personality issues, guaranteed. The manager is seen as the tool of the landlord, a phenomenon which is magnified significantly when a family member of the owner is installed in that role, especially a child. If your children are in need of housing, it is wiser to rent another apartment somewhere else than to install one or more of them in your income property.

In my experience, on-site managers can become bossy and punitive, which is the nature of the beast, not necessarily because the people involved are ill-intentioned. Placing another in such a place of responsibility also removes you from the loop because you have no way of finding out when problems arise, especially personality clashes, which can result in the loss of tenants, and thus, revenue.

The manager won't tell you there is a problem because he wants to keep his position, or he will exaggerate the situation out of proportion. The tenant won't tell you because he would rather just move, which is usually what happens. This puts you, the landlord, smack in the middle of a schoolyard spat, where you have to be the third-party arbiter of your own property. It is far safer for your investment not to create the atmosphere to begin with, because it is a no-win situation.

The cost effectiveness of hiring a management service has to be considered. As a landlord, you are motivated to learn many repair skills you may never have thought you could, or engage those skills you may have learned in high school shop class and thought you had forgotten. It is also worth your while to find independent workmen who are willing to take care of the things you can't do, and for a reasonable price. For example, on local websites such as those of the local newspaper or TV station, Craig's List, and Angie's List, you can find tradesmen who recognize the volume of business that you can provide on a regular basis, and who are willing to work with you on services and price. As I will explain in detail later, I always had the lawns mowed for all my properties, which at times meant ten or 12 properties – including the one I live in – every two weeks. Some yards were huge, but some were the size of postage stamps. I was able to arrange, with several providers at different times, a flat fee per yard, with the understanding that the small yards made up for the large ones.

The other tradespeople who may be necessary to your operation, depending on what your own skill level is, and the time you have to make repairs, are a general handyman, a plumber, and an electrician. Many plumbing problems do not require the skill and attention of a licensed plumber; a leaky faucet may take a few minutes and a dollar's worth of parts to fix. However, you should have the number of a licensed firm handy for complicated sewer and plumbing problems, such as tree roots growing into the pipes. Any electrical repair more complicated than replacing a burned-out bulb should be handled by a licensed electrician, and it is worth the expense because a licensed electrician is insured for property damage caused by poor workmanship. Some communities require that certain repairs be done by a licensed professional anyway.

Professional management services, at first blush, may appear to be the answer to all your problems. This may be the answer if you only have one or two houses and live out of the area. However, you should be aware that management companies use their own tradespeople and often charge an override fee for arranging the service. Believing they are honor-bound to provide top-grade (translation: expensive) service, the company will send a licensed plumber to fix the leaky sink. Of course, they have an obligation to assure you that the solution is that simple, or something direr (read: expensive), and to do less would be a dereliction. This is not ill intention in the part of the management service or their employees; this is how they make their living.

To every rule, there is an exception. If you are fortunate or astute enough to be able to purchase a building with proven on-site management and long-term tenants, take it and cherish it.

A financial play you may not have considered is to own a duplex, tripex, or quadraplex using one unit as your homestead. The Department of Veterans Affairs (VA) and the Federal Housing Administration (FHA) will guarantee loans for the purchase of up to four units at very favorable rates and terms, provided the borrower lives in one of them. Assuming you don't want to spend much of your life in such a unit, it nonetheless presents an excellent choice for those just starting to build their financial portfolio, or those retiring who want to stretch their housing dollars into an excellent income.

If you choose to purchase a duplex, for example, with the intention of living in one side and renting out the other, you can enjoy fantastic tax advantages, as well as the obvious offset against the mortgage that the rented unit will bring. Not only can you write off the mortgage interest for both units, you can also depreciate the rental unit, which is not allowed on an owner-occupied unit, and you can offset all of the expenses from the rental unit against your taxes, as well. In all probability, you will be able to realize a comfortable profit from a third, and even fourth unit.

This plan works well for those just starting out because they can save most, if not all, of their monthly rental expenses while they are able to begin to save appreciable amounts of money and still maintain a comfortable lifestyle. When a person in this situation is ready for a single-family home, the now-vacated unit can be rented out, and the amounts saved from not having to pay rent can be used as a down payment for a home. This actually works out quite well.

For folks who are retired and are on a fixed income, managing the property they live in can provide a rewarding investment of time and can provide housing at virtually no cost, or with an income which can maintain or improve living circumstances. Retirees may be able to take advantage of property tax deferments and other benefits; a tax professional can offer more guidance.

A mortgage broker is qualified to assist in arranging financing using these vehicles. Loan brokers who work in this area often have other kinds of loans which may prove to be even more beneficial at the time you want to buy.

With the exception of my homestead, where I want the comfort of a 30-year fixed mortgage – a quirk I developed many years ago for no special reason – virtually all of my income properties have been seller-financed. For our purposes here, there are certain criteria within the building itself which should go into the consideration of whether or not to make the purchase.

My one absolute requirement is that each unit have its own utility meters in states where utility companies cannot lien property for non-payment by anyone other than the owner. For example, in Texas, the tenant can contract with utility companies directly for services. Because each unit has a separate meter, the utility will bill the tenant. If the tenant fails to pay the bills, the landlord isn't responsible and the property can't incur a lien or be sold for non-payment. In fact, the utility companies may not talk to you because the account is not in your name. You cannot turn the utilities off in an effort to convince a tenant to move out, which is an option in some jurisdictions if you pay the bills. However, on balance, the advantages of having the tenant take responsibility for payment are so far superior that it is fundamental in all my rentals.

Other states, such as Oklahoma, allow utility companies to lien property for non-payment of utility bills; the landlord almost has to pay the utilities to eliminate the risk of losing his property because a tenant doesn't pay his bills. Of course, the rent includes utilities, but the landlord must now find another way to screen tenants, and the landlord must pay the bills whether the tenant pays his rent or not.

Assuming you can require the tenant to take responsibility for the utilities, the vast majority of your screening chores are done automatically, with virtually no cost to you.

Don't mention payment of utilities in your ads. When a prospect answers your ad and asks if the rent includes the bills, your answer of "no" will, almost always, result in a suddenly-uninterested person who can't get off the phone fast enough. No wonder. If a prospective tenant needs to have his bills paid by the landlord, he may have a poor credit history with the utility companies. Most utility companies do an excellent job of screening their customers for creditworthiness, and you are certainly free to take advantage of this fact. Their methods are better than any service you can buy to accomplish the same thing.

If the prospective tenant is a first-timer, such as a new graduate just starting out, a young couple in their first home, or people in similar circumstances, he may not have a poor history, but he may have to pay a sizable deposit to establish service, to guarantee that payment will be made responsibly.

While that deposit is not paid to you, it is nonetheless just as good. The tenant has invested in the rental, which is where you want him. Most utilities refund the deposit (or, more likely, apply it to future bills) after a period of satisfactory payment, but in any event, you win. If this type of tenant gets off to a bad start, he will not only be unable to pay the utility bills, but he won't be able to pay the rent, either. Then you can evict, the utility company keeps its deposit, and you keep yours. Hopefully, this won't be the case, but as the landlord, you are protected against unnecessary risk.

Once in a while, a prospective tenant without good utility credit will talk a friend or relative with good credit into putting the utilities in her name. If that person wants to maintain good credit, she will help the tenant pay the bills, even if the tenant is not able to pay the rent. If it is a relative, there is probably some assistance with the rent if the finances become a problem, or the tenant will default, in which case you can evict, but this has been a rare occurrence in my experience.

The ability of a tenant to pay his own utilities is the most objective way to screen for the tenants you are looking for. Since you don't pay the bills, you can't rent to the one who is looking for you to do so, and you can give an objective reason not to rent without going through a confrontation. It is the most efficient way to separate the creditworthy from those you don't want to bankroll for the better part of the month. Even better, the old game of living off the landlord until the rent is due is cut off from the beginning. When the landlord gets the utility bills he pays whether the tenant pays the rent or not; if the tenant has to take responsibility for his own usage, this is averted.

If all the prospective tenant cares about is that you pay the bills, find a reason to pass because he's probably not someone you want to spend a lot of time on. Someone who asks as an afterthought or if you are the one to make the offer is probably someone worth your attention.

As with everything else, there are exceptions. Every once in a while, a young person about to flee the nest will follow his world-wise parents' sound advice and ask if the rent includes the utilities.

A conversation on economic realities usually clears up any misconceptions. After asking pointed questions about his ability to qualify for utility services, I would tell the caller that "This is America, where there is no such thing as a free lunch." This usually elicited a laugh, which gave me the opportunity to continue. I explained that if I paid the bills, I would have no choice but to take the highest expense in any month and add it to the rent to cover the costs, whether the utility service was used or not. Not only did the prospect usually come around, but I felt good because I was able to teach a lesson in personal responsibility. "If I pay the bills, you won't think twice about blasting the air conditioner all day, whether you're there or not. If you have to pay for it, you'll learn to shut it off before you leave." The point is, it's much cheaper for the tenant if he regulates his own usage and pays his own bills. It also means the energy-conscious tenant doesn't have to subsidize the guy who likes to live in a meat locker. Very rarely did the well-meaning parents prevail, but that was okay, too.

I had one exception to the separate-meter rule. For some unknown reason, water tends to have a common meter, even though other utilities are individual to the unit. In such a case, I took the highest usage for the year, divided it by the number of units, divided again by 12 months, and added it to the rent. This also took into account the inevitable clean freak who thought that since water was "free", he may as well wash every square inch of his pickup truck every weekend, rain or shine, with gallons of wasted water streaming into the gutter.

The downside to paying for the water is that tenants will let a sink drip or a toilet run and just get used to the noise. When the tenant pays the bills, believe me, you hear about the leaky sink. If you pay the bills, the only way you will find out about the leaky sink is when you get an unusually high water bill. Lest you get the impression that it can't cost that much, I'm here to tell you that one running toilet can sink your whole ship! One tenant didn't report a running toilet because he thought it was "just normal toilet noises," which ran the bill from $80 per month for five units to well over $1000 in a single month. It does not hurt to periodically remind tenants to report water leaks, or to check for yourself from time to time.

If you are renting out a single-family residence, make sure to find someone who likes to garden, although I still found it prudent to arrange for lawnmowing service, for the sake of the neighbors if nothing else. The tenant could trim trees or tend to a vegetable garden, but if he gets tied up at work, the lawn goes untended.

Chapter 2: What is a Landlord?

There is a fallacy that landlords and tenants are as natural enemies as bugs and flyswatter; that they have opposite interests that are destined to collide. The stereotypical landlord must be ever-vigilant to ensure that the tenant is always on his best behavior, and conversely, the tenant really wants to be left alone in the property he has rented and would like to make a home.

After renting more than 50 units to more than 500 tenants as a small investor/owner, the one attitude I have always insisted upon in dealing with prospective tenants, tenants, and former tenants is that it must be assumed that all parties are acting in good faith at all times. Assuming the worst about the folks who are buying what you are offering, and feeling that you have to be vigilant to protect yourself from "them", is self-defeating.

It is much more fruitful all the way around if you don't see your market as "them", but rather, as "us". You have property to rent out and your tenant needs a home. Very, very few tenants have let me down or have swayed me from this philosophy.

What if the landlord has assumed that the tenant is justified in his desire for a home which reflects his personal tastes, and what if the tenant assumed that the landlord wants the tenant to stay a while in a comfortable environment, invites creativity, and doesn't mind nail holes in the walls? (It's easier to spackle a nail hole than it is to scrape off that green putty, and for that reason, I don't allow the green putty. What's one rule among friends?)

Even further, what if the landlord assumed that the tenant had a stake in protecting the landlord's property as if it were his own? And what if the landlord had a philosophy of *mi casa es su casa* and invited the tenant to enjoy the use of the property without the landlord looking over his shoulder?

Why, this would turn the fractious relationship between these two on its ear! The earth might be thrown off its axis, the sun might rise in the west, and it might snow in Texas in July!

What does this mean, in practical terms? These folks need each other. They still have opposite needs and wants, but each side can have what it wants without infringing upon each other. It's a true win-win situation.

There is another fallacy, that there are "good" and "bad" neighborhoods, and that tenants who can afford the former are more likely to take care of the property and are, therefore, more desirable (both property and tenant), and that the same is not true of the latter. Having owned both, and having rented to both, I have come to the realization that neither of these conclusions is true (or fair) when you make it worth the tenants' while.

Chapter 3: Business is Business – Keeping the Tenant at Arm's Length

Landlords tend to find themselves at opposite ends of two extremes: Either they seek out tenants who feel like family, including actual family members, or they become so protective of their property that no one can meet their expectations. These latter types have taken to heart the horrendous stories about tenants trashing property for the fun of it. Another is to stick the landlord with three months' rent because the landlord has too big a heart to demand rent over Christmas, especially when the tenant has children. Why should the kids suffer because the parents are deadbeats, and besides, it is reasonable to spend the rent money on good gifts.

Ownership of rental property can be a steady, reliable source of income with an outstanding return on investment, or it can be a bottomless financial and emotional pit. I'm here to tell you that it is all within the exclusive control of the landlord.

Let me repeat that. Whether you make money providing quality housing for tenants you respect and enjoy, or find yourself with a strong desire to find a match to light at the earliest opportunity, is exclusively within your control.

There are certain truisms that should be taken at face value. People are remarkable creatures of habit and will react – not act, but *react* – with complete predictability and will always, *always* act in his own self-interest when it is worth his while to do so. You do not have to sacrifice your morals and values, and you do not have to be muscular or demanding. You simply have to structure your agreements so that the tenant finds it worthwhile to act in your best interest because he sees it as his best interest, because it is. This is known as a win-win situation and it sure makes life easier for everyone.

The first rule is that this is a business. Even if you came into the property through inheritance, donation, or default without your conscious consent, you must always treat it like a business. You have a capital investment, you've attracted interest from your prospective tenant, and your prospective tenant has taken steps toward renting from you by responding to your promotion by contacting you and making an appointment.

The second rule is that you will never rent a property over the telephone. That is not the purpose of the contact. The contact is to establish a mutuality of understanding about the property in terms of location, price, features, and the like, which, if acceptable to the prospect, might lead to a successful conclusion. The purpose of the contact is to set up an appointment based on expression of a further interest in taking the next step.

Let's assume that you can further this prospect toward a successful conclusion because you have already established, through the initial conversation, that this person can pay his own utilities, thus making him creditworthy.

Remember, this is a business relationship: you have attracted interest from someone who needs what you are offering. The prospect has expressed a need by looking in a newspaper, at a website, or through some other source; he has narrowed his search by price, size, and features, and has taken the action of calling for the purpose of finding information that wasn't listed in the paper, such as the address, *which you should never, ever publish*. So far, so good. Your investment in the ad, even if it's just the time spent composing and posting it online, has the ability to pay off by turning the prospect into a rent-paying tenant.

No one ever rented property over the phone even with Skype, and if anyone ever wants to do that, you should raise an eyebrow about his motives. In order to have the chance to complete the transaction, the prospect has to see the property. You should always meet the prospect at the property, and by all means, you should never, ever meet the prospect at your home or office. As an example, the property for rent could be in a fine part of town with pretty trees and wide, well-kept lawns, but the areas between your off-site meeting place and the property for rent may be in the parts of town that don't look so nice. If the prospect follows you to the property, he is likely to remember the not-so-pretty parts, regardless of how the property shows.

Never publish the address of the property in your promotional materials or advertising, for several reasons. You risk creating traffic of unaccompanied window shoppers, which creates a nuisance for your current tenants. People with a newspaper or a Craig's List printout think nothing of knocking on the door of a current tenant to ask questions, invading both the current tenant's privacy and possibly that of a former tenant, if the lookie-loo goes in that direction. Even if the prospective tenant rents the unit, the current tenant he bothered may have an unfavorable impression, creating a negative relationship from the start.

The person knocking on the door may not even be a prospective tenant, but someone you don't want hassling your tenants, such as a skip tracer, a door-to-door sales rep, or a burglar looking for occupied units. And don't forget that the Internet is forever. It's a fantastic place to advertise for tenants, but an ad may linger on a website long after the place is rented. Having the address in the listing all but guarantees that people will show up because they don't know it's been rented, but if a prospect has to call, you can tell him that that unit was already rented, and you have the opportunity to bring up other units you may have open. This way, the new tenant won't be bothered in his new home and you don't have to pass up on a prospect.

Meeting the tenant also gives you the opportunity to show the unit in its most favorable light. You will want to come a little early to freshen the place up, to make sure the electricity is turned on, and to make sure any trash is picked up. It gives you the opportunity to show off features that may not be obvious to someone looking through the window, which is especially true of older buildings that may not have much curb appeal.

And, of course, the very act of calling about the ad and setting up an appointment to see the apartment says that the prospective tenant is motivated to look and willing to rent. He may even bring his checkbook with him. Use this opportunity to show him that his time and money are well-spent.

If your schedule does not allow you to show the property during daylight hours, arrange to meet the tenant the same evening. I discovered there is an advantage to immediacy; do not set appointments for a future date if you can avoid it. Most people looking at rental property have an immediate need to look, decide, rent, and move. Only if the prospect is coming in from out of town did I have much success with pre-arranging showings. Often, the prospect forgets the appointment or finds something else and does not have the courtesy to cancel, or I have already rented the apartment to someone with his checkbook already in hand.

I have never held an apartment for rent off the market without a firm cash deposit to do so. Of course, the longer the prospect took to make up his mind, the less likely he was to get much of the deposit back. I can't recall a single incident when a prospect came back to rent the apartment when I held it off the market without a deposit. The prospect has to be told that you have the property advertised for rent; that you are looking for a suitable tenant for the property; and that you simply cannot hold the property for him without a deposit. This is an arrangement separate and apart from any other arrangement you may enter with the prospect unless you agree to apply the deposit if the deal is completed.

When making the appointment to show the property, make sure you have the correct address and provide specific directions, including landmarks. If there are multiple ways to approach the property, pick the one most pleasing to see. That said, many people use a GPS of some kind to navigate. Make sure you give the exact street address so the prospect can go to the right place.

If you have to show the property at night, make sure the electricity is turned on during the time the apartment is vacant. The tenant may ask about utility costs. My stock answer was that, since I didn't pay the bills, I would not be the best source of information, and that the utility company would be able to tell him exactly what the usage and bills of the previous tenants were. The prospect usually asks about those details after he has made the decision to rent. Seldom have utility expenses discouraged a prospective tenant from renting the property once he has decided to rent it.

Probably the best investment a landlord can make today is a smart phone so you and your prospective tenant can talk and text. Modern technology has made answering machines passe and many people don't have the patience to wait for a return call. The plain truth is that most people won't even leave a message. It's far easier to make an appointment with someone who answers the phone immediately, or who can accept and send text messages.

The prospect you so carefully nurtured will just rent from the guy who thinks the prospect's business is important enough to respond immediately. A business card with a phone number, fax number, e-mail address, and cell phone number is, in my experience, a bit much. That much information on a card is confusing; if you want people to get in touch with you, you need to make it as easy as possible to do so.

From the prospective tenant's viewpoint, there are so many considerations that enter into his decision whether or not he wants to rent from a particular landlord, or has particular circumstances that you must be prepared for anything. Sometimes the prospect may not even know the reasons behind those feelings, but I think it's important to look at the psychology of what turns a prospect into a tenant.

Most potential tenants know the landlord is putting his best foot forward, but he is concerned about how the landlord will follow through once the deal is sealed. Being immediately available by phone or text is an advantage to a good ongoing working relationship. The tenant wants assurances that the landlord will be available to take care of anything that comes up. Not too many tenants are thrilled with having to leave a voice mail and to wait for a call back if a pipe breaks.

If you are not comfortable with the idea of using your private cell number as a business phone, you do have a couple of options. The first is to get a line added to your existing account and carry a second phone. If this doesn't do anything for you, consider getting a Google Voice or Vonage account and downloading the app to your current phone. This will give you a second, separate phone number that you can use in your advertising. I have always carried a cell for business, but my daughter uses Google Voice for her business and it works quite well for her. She does recommend, however, using a separate ring tone for tenants so you know you have to answer those calls; if you use Google Voice or Vonage, a separate ring tone for *those* calls is a good idea, as well.

Every suggestion made here is intended to give prospective tenants that the landlord won't disappear once the deposit has been paid and the keys have been handed over. The condition of the property and the consistency of the landlord in the way he does business reassures the prospective tenant that what he sees is what he will get. A promise that doesn't have to be made is a promise that can't be broken. Miscommunications and misunderstandings usually create more hard feelings than any other aspect of the landlord/tenant relationship. Therefore, it makes sense not to get involved with situations that will be misinterpreted.

I learned that the landlord gains absolutely no advantage to showing a rental unit before the departing tenants have moved out. I do not advertise an apartment for rent until it has been cleaned and repaired.

The best way to explain to a prospective tenant what his rent is buying is to show him. Making sure the unit is clean and in good condition not only shows the prospect what you have to offer, but gives a subtle message that you expect him to take care of the property. It shows that you take pride in your product, and that you respect the prospect enough to give him the best you can offer. There are some prospects that won't be satisfied no matter how clean the apartment is. You can promise not to charge for any improvements he may choose to make once he decides to rent the place. You would be amazed at how many prospective tenants jump at the chance to improve their space because so many landlords do not allow for creativity.

I have had amusing situations when the tenant and I have had to have a conversation with a judge about the necessity of paying rent, which is my diplomatic way of saying that the tenant is a deadbeat who won't pay the rent for whatever reason, forcing me to file for eviction. Invariably, the tenant in such a situation will defend his actions by claiming the apartment was a pit when he rented it. The judge's response was that this tenant was obviously an individual of impeccable taste who would never compromise his standards to rent a home in the condition just described.

Having the property in an attractive, rentable condition also discourages prospective tenants from offering to make the property ready for occupancy in exchange for a rent reduction or deposit waiver. You have priced your rental property based on the market conditions for similar properties in best rentable condition, as well as your opinion of its location, amenities, and so forth. Under no circumstances should you lower your requirements. The exception is if it does not rent at your set price after three successive prospects have turned it down, then you probably need to reassess and fix, clean, deodorize or...well, just fix it, but don't lower the rent. unless the market has dropped for reasons beyond your control.

Giving the opportunity to work off the deposit is asking for trouble. What do you do if he fails to live up to his end of the bargain? What if there is a misunderstanding about the nature of the work to be done? Who pays to correct the work to your standards? The examples are endless, but it should be clear that the only guarantee in this scenario is ambiguity, and that cannot end well. If none of these items are even options, then by definition it cannot be ambiguous. By offering the property as you want it from the first time the prospect sees it, then he can take it as is, or he can decline.

Few prospects are honest enough to tell you "I don't like this place because..." Usually, they give you a lame excuse and assurances they will get back you; usually, you never hear from them again. On the other hand, if you give him the opportunity to be honest about what he doesn't like about the apartment, he will usually welcome it but don't try to save this prospect. Chances are, if he saw a problem, others did, too. It could be anything from a peculiar odor to a poorly-done paint job. It could be something as simple as the unit or neighborhood not meeting the prospect's needs. For example, if the prospect works nights, he probably doesn't want to share a wall with a family that has young children.

Thank the prospect for his honesty, send him on his way, and fix the problem, if there is one. If you have rented the property at that price before, the next prospect to see it should take it.

Avoid the temptation of presenting all the vacancies you have to a prospect, and do not do a generic or "gang" ad because the more choices a prospect has, the less likely he will be to pick one. If you have multiple units to rent, pick one unit to concentrate on and leave the rest until you are ready to do it right. Once you know what you're doing, getting an apartment ready should take a minimum of time. Depending on what you have available at any given time, descriptions, locations, and other pertinent information will be different. If properly written, each ad will differ enough that vacancies are not interchangeable, anyway. Even if you have two vacancies at the same location, do not give the tenant the choice. Stick to the one which first attracted him, and keep with that one until it's rented, then start on the rest.

You have already screened this prospect through his ability to pay utility bills. He then sets an appointment to view the property in person. You have made the effort to ensure that the grounds are clean and neat, that the property looks clean from the street, and that the unit and building smell pleasant, with carpets in good condition, polished wood, and so forth; this is to make sure the image in the tenant's mind matches the reality. He knows that you did not exaggerate, and if anything, that the unit is better than he could have imagined.

In order to maintain an ongoing positive relationship with your tenants, you cannot afford to let your position as the landlord be seen as personal. If a tenant needs help paying the rent, find a business-like solution. Some tenants believe that the rent can take a back seat to other obligations. As the landlord, you need to be clear that the rent is an obligation that must be paid on time. You do not need to make excuses for why this is, but you do need to remain firm and business-like. If your tenants think of you as their friend, they will expect you to be understanding toward their financial problems and that you will allow the rent to slide a few extra days while they sort things out.

People generally don't take advantage to be difficult. Everyone has to make choices about how she spends her money. `If the tenant sees you as a kind, understanding friend, he may decide you'll be okay if the rent is paid a little late. If a businesslike relationship has been established from the start, and if the boundaries that go along with that are enforced and respected, the tenant will understand that you do mind if the rent is late, and that arrangements had better be made.

This means that you should be understanding – after all, you've probably been in the same situation as your tenant – and flexible. Perhaps the tenant is chronically late because his paydays don't always line up with the day the rent is due, or that he can afford the rent, but that splitting the rent into two payments each month will make things easier on his cash flow. If the same tenant is coming to you regularly asking to push the rent back a few days, you might want to see if an alternative arrangement will work better. For example, moving the due date so it lines up, or agreeing to a split payment if it comes from the tenant's bank bill pay service, may make the difference having to approach the tenant regularly for overdue rent and having a more relaxed relationship.

You might need to ask some guiding questions to see what the issue really is, and you must be willing to be flexible. You are in business to make money, after all, and an occupied apartment will make more money than a vacant one will. If you are willing to work with your tenants, you will also enjoy a good reputation, something you need if your buildings are in a college, military, or some other one-horse town. When my daughter went to college, her classmates learned quickly through the grapevine which landlords were worth renting from and which weren't. The good ones had waiting lists for their apartments, while the bad ones rented to kids whose only alternative was to live in the dorm. And some felt that dorm life was preferable and another apartment stood vacant for the year.

Above all, you and your tenant must be crystal-clear in what the expectations are, and what the tenant is able to do. If the rent is due on the 1st, and you ask the tenant if he can pay it on the 10th, he may feel cornered and tell you what he thinks you want to hear. On the other hand, if you ask the tenant when he can pay it, he will likely be more honest. You might also ask him if he needs a day or two after that. When that discussion is over, make sure you and he are clear on the final outcome, that the due date going forward has now been changed to the 15th of the month. The discussion, while difficult, will make the tenant feel better about coming to you with any further problems, and that you will work with him. Any ambiguities are not going to end well, and you will probably end back where you started, with a tenant who still doesn't pay the rent on time.

Chapter 4: A Contract is a Contract is a Contract (sort of)

After spending many very hot Texas afternoons cleaning up after former tenants who had renter's remorse for whatever reason – usually, due to my failure to relax my expectations that the rent be paid on time – it occurred to be that there had to be a better way for a committed lazy person like me to get around all the extra physical labor.

Tenants who did not like the leases I spent hours drafting, or who decided that they didn't like their neighbors, who had also signed leases with me, or lost jobs and could no longer afford the rent, felt that the best course of action was to pack up and move out in the middle of the night. Some thought it would serve me right to trash the apartment, as though the sudden vacancy wasn't enough of a statement.

Not only were these units trashed, but I often didn't find out about the sudden vacancy until the rent didn't show up. Common sense might dictate that the neighbors would mention something, but in all the years that I've owned income property, I can't remember one tenant calling to report that someone else had moved out.

Once I found out that the tenant had moved out, I had to go in and clean the place. More often than not, the power would be shut off, leaving the unit without air conditioning or a working refrigerator. I would be greeted by the smell of food rotting in the refrigerator, garbage decaying in the hot apartment, and Lord knows what else that had been left behind. I'd have to open every window in the place, run a fan to vent the smell, then get to work.

You may ask why I didn't know that these people had moved out. I made it my business to go by each of my properties at regular, but unpredictable intervals. I never entered a tenant's home without an invitation to do so. I may own the property, but the space my tenants rent belongs to them. I also don't discuss one tenant's business with another; if he really wants to know, I figure he can ask. I can't get into trouble for what I don't talk about, and talking out of school is an invitation for trouble. My tenants' business is theirs, and I have no legal or moral right to invade their space or their lives.

There are a few exceptions to this policy. The first are emergencies. If a tenant isn't home and the pipes burst, I'm not going to wait around for him to get home to get permission to enter the apartment. The other covers reasonable notice for a defined purpose, such as an inspection or for landlord-needed repairs. Of course, it's optimal if the tenant can be there, but that's not always possible.

Even if you suspect that the tenant has moved out, you do not have the right to enter the property without a reason and without reasonable notice. The fastest and easiest way is to call the electric company and ask if the power is still on. Some utility companies will send a notice to the owner of the property if service has been disconnected, so you will get a heads-up, but not all do. Some will also leave a notice on the door. Not all utilities do these things, so you may have to call to ask if there is still electricity at the property.

There are legal possession issues if you learn the power is not on, or if there is a shutoff order. If the power has been turned off, you can declare the property "abandoned". An apartment with no power is uninhabitable, and because it is uninhabitable, you can make claim and enter the unit without having to get a court order. While this is true in Texas, it may not be the case in other jurisdictions, so you want to check with local laws to find out how to proceed. In other words, it is possible that the landlord could be considered guilty of trespassing on his own property because in exchange for the rent, he has given up the right to its use to another and has, therefore, waived his right to enter the property at will.

All of this assumes the worst possible scenario, that you end up feeling foolish because you feel the tenant took advantage, something most try to avoid at substantial cost. If you assume that everyone, including the landlord, acts in his own best interest, not necessarily consciously or maliciously, then the best solution is to make the tenant's interest the same as yours.

A little bribery goes a long way as a motivating force; it revolutionizes the historical theory that landlords and tenants are at odds with each other. If strategically applied, tenants are encouraged to do the right thing by you and your property.

I have to give a history of how I came to realize this, and if you think about it, you've probably experienced this same thing. It occurred to me that the reason I was having so many problems with tenants not living up to the terms of their leases is because most people don't understand what a lease is. They don't see it as an agreement between two parties, they see it as a Legal

Document (emphasis mine) which has the ability to consume them like a boa constrictor. As a result, many sometimes feel that the only way to avoid lifelong ruin and bad reputation is to sneak out in the middle of the night.

Adding to the confusion of what security from a good tenant is, most landlords also do not understand this document. Both parties are under the impression that once a lease is signed, it's embedded into concrete. I've even been accused by disgruntled tenants for breaking the law because I avoided formal written leases. Of course, it's not a crime not to have a self-contained, written lease. Can you imagine the clog that would create in our criminal justice system?

Simply stated, a *lease* is an agreement between two parties for the exclusive use of the subject of the lease for a specified period of time. This could be for a car, a horse, a computer, warehouse space, or turkey hunting rights. It is nothing more nor less than an agreement where the *lessor* (the landlord or his agent) agrees to give up the use of his property to the *lessee* (the tenant) *for a determinable period of time* in exchange for a fee called *rent*. That's all it is. The rest of the multipage document is nothing more than fine print that describes a lot of what-if situations in the event both sides don't quite see eye-to-eye.

The landlord is under the impression that if it is in writing, he's got the tenant where he wants him, which is supposed to protect him against the tenant's indiscretions, whatever those happen to be. The tenant, on the other hand, gets that sinking feeling that he just signed his firstborn child away.

Did you ever notice the blank space on pre-printed residential leases which require the total amount of rent due for the term of the lease? In my experience, virtually all prospective tenant budgets are built on a month-to-month basis. While the figure on that line is divided by the months in the term and is thus payable monthly, seeing such an astronomical figure in writing will reduce even the strongest-of-heart to faint in a puddle of his own sweat.

The tenant, needing a place to live and seeing no alternative, will sign that intimidating document. At that point the tenant's attitude changes as he tries to make sense of your obligations to him, and what he can expect from you.

Many years ago, my father inherited a fourplex residential building. He believed that he was obligated to respond immediately to his tenants' requests and consequently spent many nights snaking the plumbing of one of the tenants who liked to shower at three in the morning. I think this woman had the hots for Daddy, but she'd call at 3:10 and he'd be over to rescue her by 3:30. His incessant griping caused by lack of sleep leads me to believe that he did not feel the same about her. The experience so turned him off of owning rental property that he sold the building as fast as he could, despite its being a good building in a nice part of town, and probably worth a fortune today. She expected him to be there at 3:30 a.m., snake in hand, and he felt obligated to live up to her expectation. This is an extreme example, but there are landlords who believe that the lease obligates them to respond to all their tenants' requests, no matter how unreasonable, and tenants, who believe their leases entitle them to this level of service.

The solution is to remove the lease from the equation altogether. Believe it or not, a formal, written document is not necessary to have a binding agreement between the parties. Even a pre-printed residential rental forms are written by lawyers who represent landlords, not tenants. While these documents contain certain language against the landlord because it's legally required, it still boils down to this: The landlord agrees to provide housing and the tenant agrees to pay for it. It really is no more complicated than that.

Due to a lengthy history of landlord abuses against tenants, states enacted laws to protect tenants. Where there is discretion in the wording favoring one side or another, the landlord's attorney, naturally, is going to weight those clauses in favor of the landlord. This means that tenants may be giving up rights, unknown to them, which only gives the landlord ways to collect money if the tenant defaults in some way.

This is a good thing, the landlord might say, because he gains advantages he would not have otherwise. Not so. The law assumes that the landlord will take advantage of the tenant whenever he can, and that each party must protect itself against the other. Perhaps no other subject matter in the realm of interpersonal relationships has taken up so much time and attention to the most minute detail as this subject.

Note that I didn't say not to put anything in writing. I just said to eliminate the lease. To be enforceable, a contract does not have to be contained on one piece of paper as long as the intent of the parties is clear. You can hitch several pieces of paper together, which taken as a whole, shows what you and the tenant intend.

By giving the tenant a receipt at the time he tenders his money, you create a written agreement which will protect your interests in any court in this land.

Remember, I said it is counterproductive to have a formal, written lease agreement with a tenant because the formality of the document itself is so unnecessarily intimidating. That doesn't mean that you don't have a written agreement. Many think that in order to be binding and enforceable, a contract must be contained within one document. This is not true. You can have as many documents as you need, as long as you can show what both parties intended.

A duplicate receipt book can replace a formal written, intimidating lease when it contains blanks for the date, the name of the tenant, the address of the property, the method of payment (cash, check, etc.), two or three non-specific blanks, and a signature line for you or your agent.

In order to create a binding agreement, you need:

- The date of the agreement
- The address of the property being rented, including the unit number
- The date the rental is to begin
- The length of time the rent is being paid for, usually every 30 days, which creates a month-to-month rental, which renews every month until one or the other party gives notice
- The signature line, indicating that you accept the terms of the agreement.

When the tenant makes out a check to you or hands over cash, he assents to the terms.

The deposit should be entered as a separate item, and specified that it is a deposit. This amount should be different from the monthly rent amount so there is no confusion later. For example, if the rent is $400 a month, make the deposit $350 or $500.

Regardless of what a pre-printed list may say, deposit refunds are one of those things that have specific legal requirements. If you research nothing else about the legal obligations of being a landlord, make it your business to learn every aspect of deposit refunds. In Texas, for example, the landlord has 30 days in which to assess and repair legitimate damages, and return the difference along with a specific accounting for how the deposit was spent. If the refund is made on the 31st day, there are treble damages, the deposit itself, plus $100 just to make the point. I learned the hard way when a deposit of $175, all of which would have gone to damages, turned into a judgment against me for $800 plus court costs.

The tenant may ask if he can pay the deposit later or if he can work off the deposit by doing chores or keeping the yard. Or he may offer to take the apartment before you clean it up instead of paying a deposit. Don't do it. The deposit is not only to ensure the tenant's performance, it gives you a psychological edge with the tenant. He has paid that money not only to guarantee his performance, but yours, at least in his head.

In some states, you are required by law to keep deposit funds in a separate account, which you can only transfer after the tenant has moved out and the expenses have been accounted for on separate ledgers. In others, you can keep the deposit and rent money in a single account. In Texas, for example, it is perfectly acceptable to put deposits and rent in the same account, without having to keep a separate accounting. Even if you're not required to keep a separate ledger, using a program like Excel or Google Sheets makes accounting easier. From a tax perspective, deposits are not taxable until it is determined that you are entitled to compensation from those funds. Check with your tax professional about the necessary documentation.

I accepted a partial deposit on two occasions, and learned lessons from both of them. When tenants are given the option to pay the deposit at a later date, it never gets paid. I can state that with absolute certainty.

I'm not insensitive to the fact that moving is an expensive proposition, and I surely would rather have the tenant than not, so it is worth my while to find a reasonable solution to the deposit dilemma. I discovered that, while tenants will virtually never make good on a promise to cover a deposit, they will always pay the rent. Under these circumstances, I would tell the tenant that I had to have the deposit now, but that I could accept half the month's rent now with the second half due in two weeks. I also emphasized that we both agreed that our arrangement was still a month-to-month rental.

Even if half the month's rent equaled the whole deposit, I always got the former and never got the latter for the same amount of money. In these cases, I would tell the tenant that if he preferred to pay the rent twice a month, that would be fine, but that there would be an extra $10 service charge for the extra book work. More frequent payments were not possible. I often rented to tenants who stayed for years on the twice-a-month basis, which worked out well for both of us.

The trick that worked best for me was the bonus I offered to pay the tenants if certain conditions were met when they moved out.

If you recall, I originally had a problem with tenants not informing me of their decision to move, and of leaving the property a disaster zone. I figured there had to be a better way. It occurred to me that if I made it financially worth the tenants' while, we would both benefit.

While the informal rental agreement was technically month-to-month, I explained that if the tenant stayed in the apartment for at least six months (one year in a condo or single-family home), gave me 30 days' notice, gave a forwarding address in writing, was entitled to receive his entire deposit, and if the unit was left in move-in condition, I would pay a bonus of anywhere from $50 to $100 in addition to the deposit. Since I had to pay someone to clean the apartment before I could rent it out again, it seemed reasonable to me to pay the tenant instead, who would then have the incentive to leave the apartment in as good a shape as he found it when he moved in. If the tenant failed to meet any of these conditions, the bonus would not be paid. This approach was so popular that it effectively ended my career as a maid, painter, and carpet shampooer. It was my pleasure to pay out the bonus and most tenants earned it. The trick here is to make sure the standards required to earn the bonus were not too difficult to reach, and to keep your word.

In order to avoid confrontation and ambiguity, I never inspected an apartment with the tenant present. Since I have a month in which to do so, I reviewed the condition of the unit after the tenant vacated, and I sent the deposit money back with the accounting to his new address. If there were any damages, I itemized them, deducted that amount from the deposit, and refunded the difference. If the tenant failed to give me his new address in writing, I would send him a certified letter at his now-former address. If he put in a forwarding address at the post office, the letter would be delivered. If not, I would get the letter back, green card and all, which gave me proof that I had made reasonable effort to reach the tenant so that I wouldn't get nailed for treble damages, the original deposit, plus $100.

I rekeyed the locks with each new tenant anyway and found it made sense to key all of the locks for any given unit the same, so the tenant only needed one key for all of the doors. Extra keys are the responsibility of the tenant.

I keep the landlords' keys on a board with hooks in my garage. I never hand keys out, even to repairpeople I trust, for their sake. Whenever possible, I ask the tenant to make arrangements with the repair people to come over when the tenant is home. My repair people are under strict instructions that anything the tenant wants over and above the necessary work is the responsibility of the tenant, and the repairman cannot do it without my express consent. I give these contractors so much business that it doesn't pay for them to do anything else.

Of course, I give out keys for vacant apartments, and I would arrange to be present at occupied units if the tenant could not be there. I don't want my repair people to have to deal with law enforcement officers in the event anything turns up missing or other complaints arise.

Many rental unit owners don't allow tenants to paint, put holes in the walls, or express themselves through décor at all. I invite my tenants to use whatever creativity they want because these are their homes. I believe that the more tenant has of himself in the place, the longer he will stay, and the more enjoyable the relationship is. They do not need my approval to make these improvements, and I must admit that I manage to find some very creative people. Not only I not charge them for these changes, but by leaving the unique flavor in the unit, I am able to command a higher rent when the tenant finally moves out. I do not contribute financially to the improvements; whatever paint, wallpaper, curtains, or other items the tenant wants, the tenant has to purchase.

Rent raises happen when new tenants move in. I never find it necessary to raise rents on tenants while they are living there, regardless of how long the tenancy lasts. My expenses are laid out based on known figures; raising the rents by a paltry amount does not make sense. Better to wait until the tenant vacates. Often, the more elaborate units which the tenants left behind allowed me to raise rents on new tenants by as much as one-third the previous rent. I discovered that prospective tenants found unique décor as delightful as the tenants who did the original work. One condo had a complete mural on two joining walls, including the light switch plates. Not only did I admire the artist, I loved the originality of the artwork.

Survival clue: When calculating damages and refunds of deposits, always refund something, and whenever possible, make it an odd amount, like

$23.12 or $5.23. I learned that if you don't send anything, the tenant is more likely to sue and then you have to justify that any repairs were not considered normal wear-and-tear, and that your expenses were not excessive. When you *refund* something, people tend not to question you and are more willing to accept whatever you say. In addition, if your tenant leaves without notice, or with short notice, you are entitled to be compensated for that time, which you may legally deduct from the deposit. Make sure you account for that expense in your final ledger to the tenant after the move-out, and within 30 days.

Chapter 5: Familiarity Breeds Contempt, or: Melting the Barriers Between Us and Them

If I have convinced you of nothing else, it's that enjoying success as a landlord comes from maintaining a professional boundary between yourself and your tenants so you both can have absolute trust in each other.

If you find yourself in the awkward position of having to rent to your relatives, then everyone concerned will be more comfortable with the arrangement if the relatives are treated no differently than any other tenant. No special concessions about rent reductions should be made.

As the landlord, you should insist that the rent be paid on time. If it isn't, then late charges should be assessed and collected, and late rent should not be accepted without the late fees. If the rent isn't paid at all because the relative has "connections", you need to be prepared to evict him, just as you would any other tenant. And in no event should you bend the rules by allowing him to work off or reduce the rent by having him "manage" the property.

When your money is invested in real estate, you need to keep control of everything, from how the property looks to prospective tenants from the street, to making sure that repair people you hire to maintain the property are doing the jobs they were hired to do. When your relationship is purely business, it's easy to fire a worker who isn't doing a good job. How do you fire your nephew? If you don't get into that position, you won't have that problem.

I rented to both my children and I believe that by enforcing a businesslike relationship, I was able to teach them the importance of taking financial responsibility for their needs, as well as an appreciation for the importance in maintaining trustworthiness in other areas of their lives. They are especially aware that landlords are not bankers who can afford to carry them when they fall a little short. They were taught to keep other tenants in mind by keeping their spaces tidy and keeping the noise down.

By the same token, as rent-paying tenants who were getting no special consideration, they had a right to insist that I do my part by keeping their properties in good repair, and that I do so in a timely fashion. This kept me on my toes and I was able to use this relationship as a laboratory for expanding working relationships with my other tenants and, most especially, in attracting prospective tenants. For example, I learned to turn a keener eye on things I might not otherwise see to make tenants happy enough to fulfill my goal of having them stay around a while.

During the times I rented to my children (actually, I rented an apartment to my daughter in a building that I owned, while I advanced my son a year's worth of rent for his fraternity house because the cash discount they offered for prepayment was too good to pass up. So, in effect, I rented the room in the frat house for which my son paid his rent on the first of each month, in effect, sub-leasing the room from me.) But the principle is the same.

I am proud to say that both children lived up to their obligations without testing my resolve, but rest assured that I was prepared to take whatever action was necessary in the event they didn't live up to expectations, and to hold them as examples to other tenants who may have thought it was okay to avoid paying the rent.

When you own multiple income units, even a duplex, tenants can harbor a resentment if they see your relatives getting special treatment that they are not getting. The rules must be consistently enforced among all your tenants, related or not. All tenants must pay the rent on time, and the landlord must keep the units in good repair on time, and trust and goodwill are inevitable.

Another boundary I found essential was never to have a tenant over to my house. Obviously, I work from there, but I make it a point never to do business there. For one thing, it's my sanctuary. For another, it leads the tenant to believe there is a closer relationship than there is, which is an invitation for the tenant to take advantage of you. For a third, it may create resentment because he is paying for your relatively lavish lifestyle. In the past, it wasn't difficult to keep tenants away, but with Google, it's somewhat harder. I also made it a point never to meet a tenant for the purposes of collecting the rent. It encourages financial irresponsibility because if I can't come by, the tenant gets extra time, and some people believe that means a little extra money.

To get around this, I got a mailbox at a private pack-and-ship place. Unlike the US Postal Service, these stores have a street address, so it's not a big deal for the tenant to drop off the rent there; the staff are usually happy to put the envelope in the box. Some of these services also forward mail to a second address for a fee, so if you do business in one place but live in another, you'll still be able to get your mail (and thus your rent money) with no problem. Finally, it encourages responsibility because the tenant has to take the initiative to mail the check or drop it off; Mohammed has to go to the mountain, not the other way around. I was always delighted when I'd open an envelope with a tenant to find a check with my property's address pre-printed on it. That meant the tenant was here to stay.

Some tenants, for whatever reason, don't have a checking account; they may pay their bills in cash or with a pre-paid debit card. Make sure that the tenant knows not to give cash to the staff at the store because they won't take responsibility for the cash, and there's no way to trace its loss if it goes missing. Encourage him to purchase a money order to pay the rent; this will give him a receipt with a tracking number. If the tenant still insists on paying in cash, make sure he knows it's at his own risk, and that it has to be in a sealed envelope.

Once the tenants moved in, I did not provide paid receipts unless a tenant asked for one, and they rarely did. When they did, I simply used a receipt from the same book as from when the tenant moved in. I put the receipt in a sealed envelope, which I dropped off at the tenant's apartment at my leisure.

Originally, I did not assess late charges because they were more trouble to keep track of than they were worth. I changed my mind when it finally occurred to me that the reason rents were coming in later and later every month was because tenants found there was no penalty for using the rent money interest-free for a few days to a few weeks.

Understanding that tenants had no bad intention when they paid the rent late, I realized that I was the one giving permission for this practice, and I had to admit that I admired tenants who were smart enough to have figured it out.

The result of my epiphany was a promise – really, a threat – to impose a specific late charge if rents were not paid within two days of the due date. I accepted responsibility for the post office by giving the doubt that the rent was in the mail. Technically, however, the tenant was in default if the rent was not paid by midnight of the due date.

Not only did rents start to appear on time without any further issue, but when a tenant expected to be a day or two late, he usually called me to tell me, and he would automatically add the late charge. It got to the point where if I found myself still having to remind a tenant to pay the rent, it usually meant trouble with the rental.

On the first go-around with late rent, I always assume the tenant sent it, but that It got lost or misdelivered or some other innocent circumstance. On the third day after the rent was due, I made it a practice to leave my business card tucked into the door frame. On the back of the card, I wrote, "rent is past due, PLEASE!" I felt an obligation to protect the privacy of the tenant, and always turned the printed side of the card out, with my name visible from the outside. If there was an honest mistake, I received a phone call almost immediately. If I didn't get a call, I prepared for Round II.

In order to prevent the possibility of any misunderstanding about promises a tenant made regarding payment of rent, I always *asked* the tenant "When can you have the rent *at the box*?" I found that when I *told* the tenant, "You will have the rent at the box by Thursday at 4:00," the tenant invariably nodded in agreement and I left myself wide open for the inevitable. If the rent did not show up by 4:00 on Thursday, the tenant would answer that I had instructed him to do so, that I had intimidated him into agreeing, but that he never said he would comply. An ambiguity had been created.

When I put the responsibility back on him by inquiring what his intentions were, the tenant couldn't easily wiggle his way out of it. When the tenant says he will have the rent at the box by Thursday at 4:00, I repeat what he says, emphasizing *the box*, the date, and the time. I found it helped improve my credibility if I asked the tenant if he needed more time, assuring him that I would go along with whatever he promised, provided he lived up to it.

The conversation told me a lot. If the tenant was flimflamming me, trying to gain a couple more days of free rent because he planned to move out without notice, I would be placed in a more favorable financial position because I could reclaim the property and re-rent it much more quickly. Time is money, literally.

In addition, I was saved the time and aggravation of taking the tenant to court to have him evicted. A tenant who is savvy about his rights can delay having to move out for up to a month, where he will be living as my guest until I can arrange to have the sheriff physically throw him into the street. I have had to do that distasteful chore twice, which is probably the hardest thing I've ever had to do as a landlord, but it's part of the business.

If the tenant legitimately needed a break, the money would be there as promised, with no further questions. As a result, the tenant and I knew we could trust each other. If a long-term tenant, for example, tell me she needed to move because she lost her job, I invited her to stay for two weeks with the understanding that the job would be replaced with another. I calculated that it would cost me two weeks' rent to make the unit ready for another tenant, and I might as well give the two weeks to a good tenant. This proved to be a good decision because the tenant got a better job and stayed quite a while longer.

Round II

Time to take the bad with the good. There are times, whether we like it or not, when tenants aren't all we hoped they would be. If you've tried the recommendations I've made here, this should be a rare occurrence, but it can still happen. Sometimes, it becomes necessary to encourage a tenant to move his troubles onto the shoulders of a more understanding landlord with whom your cast-offs might get along famously.

If the business card discreetly tucked into the front door fails to elicit a response and the rent still hasn't shown up, I would serve a "pay rent or quit" notice in his mailbox the next day. Different jurisdictions have vastly different rules for putting an eviction in motion, but all require notice to the tenant, making demand for payment by a certain date, and setting the matter for a hearing in the appropriate court.

I did not let this function lapse. On rare occasion, the 72-hour notice got the tenant's attention and he would call me to make arrangements for payment. A sample of the notice is included in the appendix. If the tenant still refuses to respond, all future correspondence should be in writing. It may be difficult to stay away from the property, but there must be no opportunity for confrontation. In an age when most people have a cell phone capable of taking photos and recording videos, you have to assume that such a confrontation will be recorded, and any words uttered (or, more likely, shouted) in the heat of passion will come back to bite you, either in court or on social media. Furthermore, you may put yourself in physical danger if the tenant or a friend of the tenant has a weapon or a devastating right jab.

So stay away until you are positive the tenant has moved out, and even then, bring someone else along when you go to check the place out afterward. If the tenant is of the type to trash the place, he will do it whether you are there or not. You will still have to clean it up, and if you are there to witness that, it might make a bad situation worse. What you can do is to take photos and video during the inspection to document the damage as evidence if it does go to court. Whatever you do, make sure you follow the absolute letter of the law, lest you find yourself on the wrong end of the court's decision.

Most tenants do not realize how much the laws in most jurisdictions favor them. I advise anyone considering becoming a landlord to rent the movie *Pacific Heights* with Matthew Modine, Melanie Griffith, and Michael Keaton as the quintessential tenant from hell. While the motive of the tenant in the movie is extreme, the laws which are discussed are all too real. The movie shows in Technicolor just how counterproductive it is to physically challenge a tenant.

Suffice it to say that it is worth your while to swallow your bile, bite your tongue, and document every single thing in writing, according to the laws of your state. It helps if you can make friends with the clerk of the court responsible for eviction actions so you don't waste time by having to start all over because of a technicality. I have found that I have not needed to hire an attorney to do this work; many people feel you need to hire one every time you have to file for eviction, but jumping in and doing it yourself once or twice to build your self-confidence would be more beneficial (and less expensive).

When written notice is served for non-payment of rent, a few move within the 72-hour deadline required by the notice. In Texas, I am able to file a forcible detainer (eviction) when the 72 hours has elapsed. As tenant-friendly as Texas is, it is relatively simple to effect an eviction. When you file your paperwork with the court and pay the fee, a hearing is set for approximately ten days after. The court may have a specific day set aside to hear landlord-tenant cases, so that may vary. The clerk can fill you in on the details of your local court's practice.

Depending on the jurisdiction, you may be able to make a claim for unpaid rent and related costs, offset by the deposit, when you file for eviction. If the tenant really trashed the place, you may have to go to court and file a separate action. Depending on the circumstances, it may be worth consulting or hiring an attorney. Whether or not you hire a lawyer, a cost-benefit analysis is crucial because in the end, it may not be worth the trouble.

As this is America, the tenant has the right to appeal. The appealing party has to post a bond, and if the tenant was put out for nonpayment of rent, he probably won't have a defense. Bonds, when set, are usually a multiple of the judgment, and many tenants tend not to want to bother with this. A tenant who knows that the landlord can't put him out of the property during the appeal period can buy that time to use the apartment.

Defenses for nonpayment of rent or a tenant's right to offset expenses against the rent are very specific. The tenant has to make reasonable demand for what he wants done in writing, it has to be reasonable, and the landlord has to be given a reasonable amount of time in which to correct the problem. If, for whatever reason, the landlord refuses to fix the problem, then the tenant can have the repairs done at his own expense and offset the costs against the rent. There may be other requirements in your jurisdiction, but your local landlord's association or attorney should have more details.

Some tenants find it prudent to move on between the time of the service of notice and the court date. Some actually move out and appear in court anyway with no defenses. However, if the tenant stays beyond the appeal deadline, then you must file yet another fee to have the constable intervene by putting the tenant's belongings off your property. This is government at its best because under the law, the tenant's belongings cannot remain on your property because that's the order from the court. It can't be placed on a neighbor's private property, and it can't be placed in the street. This unfortunate scenario doesn't usually happen, and the two times I've had to take such drastic measures, the tenants were already in the process of moving out when the constable showed up. Again, you need to be aware of the laws in your jurisdiction. In our area, you cannot put the tenant's belongings out if it's raining, which means it could be weeks until a sunny day will allow you to do so. In some cold-weather locations, you can't put a tenant out during the winter months. Also, if the tenant's belongings have to be stored, you have to hire bonded movers and transfer it to a storage locker which you have to pay for. This is truly an option to avoid. In this case, you have my permission to feel badly for the tenant; if he had the money, he would pay you. Anything beyond this is a potential movie script.

In some parts of the country, it takes months to evict someone; in others, it's illegal to evict a family with young children. For my money, this is the kind of tenant it would be easier to work with if you had agreed to pay him a bonus to move on at the time the unit was rented. For the entire deposit refund plus the bonus, you might convince the tenant to move out and clean the place up after himself.

I never lied about it, but I never gave a bad referral to another landlord. I don't believe referrals have credibility anyway, and frankly, it is embarrassing all the way around. In today's litigious society, a landlord can be sued as quickly for giving a negative reference as an employer can. Of course, the tenants I hated to see go always got glowing references, accompanied by a lament for me and kudos for the new landlord. If the reason for moving was that the tenant was leaving town, I couldn't be too sad, and have had requests of one kind or another from them for referrals many years later.

If the tenant has to be encouraged to move because of a disagreement about the necessity of paying rent, I look for positive things to say about the tenant, which usually shocks him because it's the last thing he expects. Always the cockeyed optimist, I have no way of knowing whether the tenant will click with the new landlord just because he didn't work with me. For example, if payment of rent is the problem, perhaps the rent is less expensive in the new place, which the tenant can now meet comfortably.

If I were so inclined to give a negative reference, I wouldn't do it if the tenant hadn't move out yet. If the tenant has to be asked to move on, I first assure him that my decision is not personal. I remind the tenant that I am in the business of renting property for use by others, and I am not a financial institution in a position to act as a banker for short-term money woes. I've already gone into the circumstances when I worked with the tenants rather than move them out to my detriment.

There are some who have a problem every single month. It gets tiresome and at some point, it's not worth keeping the tenant. Under these circumstances, I have written the tenant a glowing letter of recommendation for another landlord. I would never tell an untruth, but I've learned that there are ways to say things without saying them. I addressed the issue of why the tenant was moving by evading it. I would state how I hated to lose this tenant, that my loss is the new landlord's gain. I paid particular attention to the condition of the property. Of course, the tenant hadn't moved out, but in anticipation of that event, I would describe the place in such glowing terms that the tenant usually left it in the condition I described.

If the truth be known, I really feel I don't owe this landlord anything; that there are many ways to check this tenant out without my help. I never took the word of a former landlord, ever. I never asked for a reference. But beneath all that, if I gave a truthful account of the nightmare I was getting rid of, I'd be forced to keep this headache around forever. Who wants a tenant with a recommendation like that?

Once, I received a phone call looking for a reference about a tenant who had decided that her automobile mechanic had to have the rent money without discussing it with me first. Understanding that the tenant needed her car to get to work to earn the money to pay the rent, I probably would have helped her out, but it just didn't work out that way in this instance.

The new landlord went into a recitation about how badly the woman felt because, as she related it, we had had words, but other than that, what was she like, the new landlord wanted to know.

Andy, my husband, took the call. He proceeded to lay the tenant flat to the caller with her shortcomings and warnings for the landlord. He sure told the landlord, and he sure got even with the tenant, boy oh boy!

We were relatively new to the business at the time, but when Andy hung up, I said to him, "Would you rent to her with a referral like that?" "Of course not," he said. "Then why would anyone else take her? We may be stuck with her forever!" From that day on, it was every man for himself.

In choosing what words to use in my letter of recommendation, I told the truth because I hated to lose any tenant because of the promotional aspects of this business, but the tenant has always lived up to my stated image. I always referred to an eviction for nonpayment of rent as "a discussion with the judge about the necessity of paying rent" and leave it at that. I've been thanked by tenants, who even though they had to be put out, harbor no grudges.

Often, the tenant shows up in court when he has no defenses and, in fact, admits that he owes it. Once I have recited all the particulars of the agreement from my receipt book – remember, all of the elements of a contract are present, as described previously – the judge turned to the tenant and ask whether he had a defense. The answer is always no. (So why are we here, hmm?)

Once in a while, the tenant will claim that the place was a pit in he rented it and it wasn't worth the money. The wise judge earned his reputation because he always responded with "a discriminating individual such as yourself would never rent property in the condition you described." Case dismissed.

Sometimes, it's difficult to maintain a professional demeanor under these circumstances, but I always made it a point to meet with the tenant after the judgment was rendered, including not only an order to vacate the premises, but also to pay back-owed rent and court costs. At that time, I found it prudent to remind the tenant of our original agreement, by which I intended to be bound. I repeated the conditions under which he would be entitled to a refund, and I continued to stand by my bonus offer if the property was left in rentable condition. This usually resulted in better communication with the tenants, who realized that my decision wasn't personal, and that it was still worth his while to meet the challenge of the financial rewards I had promised.

At this point, a word to the wise about The Tenant Who Knows His Rights, which includes directions to the legal aid office. I'm not opposed to tenants knowing their rights; as far as I'm concerned, everyone should make it their business to know them. The tenant is, however, often wrong about his rights, and it is important to know the difference. In any event, it is much more cost effective to just get rid of the problem than to fight back on principle.

Chapter 6: Time and Aggravation Savers, or: You Knew You'd Think of It Eventually!

Landlording is surprisingly inexpensive to operate as a business, once you've bought the property.

You will need to rent a post office box where tenants drop off the rent and where you can pick it up at your leisure. You could rent a box at the local post office, but I recommend a private post office box company, such as Mailboxes Etc. or the UPS Store. As independent businesses, they offer personal service and can help in many ways. When you make use of their services, they issue you a post office box, and for mailing purposes, you can use their street address rather than a post office box. Tenants can walk in during business hours and because of the nature of the postal box business, their hours coincide with the convenience of their customers, including working people, by opening early and closing late. You may also be issued a key to gain entrance to the postal box area so you can pick up rents at your convenience, even if it means going in the middle of the night.

Finally, when you sign up for a private box, you can leave with everything you need to start using the service. If you rent a post office box from the post office, you are required to complete documentation and have to state the nature of the mail you intend to receive, which is subject to approval. Also, tenants cannot easily drop their rent check off and leave; they must pay for postage even if they drop an envelope off at the counter.

Some tenants, incredibly enough, thought I owned the store where they paid the rent and would walk in with lists of repairs or other questions, which threw the clerks at the store for a loop. You need to make sure that your tenants understand that the owner and clerks at the store have nothing to do with your business, and the staff of the store should understand that any such lists should just be put in your mailbox for you to deal with.

The next item on the list is business cards. I found that a number of places, both brick-and-mortar and online, offer 1,000 business cards for a very modest sum, if you use a pre-selected format. Of course, just as soon as you get your thousand cards, some vital information changes and you have to have them reprinted with the changes. Scratch-outs and handwritten information hurt your image, but business cards are so cheap that there's no reason not to have them reprinted. You may also print your own using pre-punched blanks. It helps to change the ink color with each run so you know you're handing out the newest version. If you are waiting for new cards to come in and have no choice but to use an old one, make the changes in front of the person and make sure they get a new one as soon as possible. Or you can print some yourself in the meantime.

A logo is probably an unnecessary expense unless you are an artist or one of your kids is, but it is a personal choice. I found that I was most comfortable with a minimum of information. I didn't use a title, but just my name in the center of the card. I added the post office box street address, including the box number, and a phone number. Later on, I added my email address, just because I had one. I made the mistake of including my fax number on one set of cards, but more people misread the card than you can imagine. It created a lot of confusion, so I reprinted my cards for the purpose of removing that number. If anyone I meet has to send me a fax, I write it in front of the person. It's a lot simpler and I don't have to worry about missing an important communication, like a late rent check, because the tenant called the fax number.

I also find that business cards are helpful for leaving notes for tenants. I keep a pile in the ashtray of my car so they're always handy, and I'm able to communicate easily by leaving notes as I make my rounds.

I cannot overemphasize the necessity of having a cell phone on you, and keeping it charged. If you have a smart phone, so much the better. Many people, especially younger people, won't leave a voice mail; they prefer to send text messages. In fact, you can use your smart phone to run your entire business if you're so inclined. In addition to its primary function as a telephone, you can:

- Take photos and videos before the tenant moves in and after he moves out to document the apartment's condition and any necessary repairs;
- Track due dates and work men visits on the calendar;
- Google repair people;
- Track mileage and expenses;
- Post electronic ads;
- Deposit checks (if your financial institution allows it);
- Calculate amounts;

- Play games or browse Facebook while you wait for people to show up.

Whatever phone you use, make sure you check messages regularly. "I don't really use my cell phone" isn't going to make a tenant feel any better if his toilet is overflowing and that's the number he has because that's the number you gave him.

Many people – and you may even be one of them – no longer have a landline and aren't comfortable using their personal cell phone number in their advertising and marketing materials. Google has a service that will assign you a separate phone number that people can call. It rings to whatever phone you tell it to, and it will allow people to leave messages or send texts. It comes with an app for your cell phone that is fairly easy to use. Since I've always had a cell phone for business, I'm okay with using it in ads, but my daughter uses Google Voice for her business and it works fairly well for her.

Tenants with a problem can become huffy when you aren't immediately reachable, and many small problems can turn into big problems if you don't respond, although this seldom happened in my experience. The ability to respond quickly is good for tenant morale and the expense of a smart phone has paid for itself many times over in the freedom it provides me. I can take care of tenants' needs immediately and I know I have gotten rentals because I'm there when the competition isn't.

If you are an old-school pen-and-paper kind of person, you're going to want to find a system that works for you. At minimum, you should have a duplicate receipt book, mileage log for tracking business-related mileage, a supply of current business cards, calculator, and pens. A spiral-bound or composition notebook works well for note-taking; the pages won't come out easily, so you can't lose any pages; if you need to write something down for someone else, use the back of a business card.

When you have established a reasonable cash flow, you may want to consider purchasing a separate vehicle solely for your business, like a pickup truck or a van. Whether you use your own car or buy another one, mileage adds up quickly and can translate into a substantial tax deduction at the end of the year. Good records are essential, because if you're audited, the IRS agent will want see documentation to justify the write-off. In fact, it's a good idea to consult with a tax professional about business deductions, especially if you've never run a business before, to reduce the risk of an audit.

There are many software programs for real estate rental business, but I have not found one with which I am comfortable. They tend to ask for information about tenants which I find to be embarrassingly personal, and none of which I would ask of anyone. When you take the position that the tenant pays the rent in exchange for your providing a roof over his head then contrary to popular opinion, invading his privacy does nothing to guarantee payment or indemnify against damages, and it is superfluous because you have given a financial incentive to pay the rent on time and to keep his place up. The only other thing you need to have from the tenant is the phone number so that you can reach someone in case the tenant has an emergency.

In my experience, tenants appreciate your not wanting to know all their business. In fact, it is silly to ask about employment because, in most jurisdictions, you can't do anything with the information anyway. You can't approach the tenant at work when the rent is late, and as long as the tenant has the rent when it's due, the rest is irrelevant. If there is the possibility of a disagreeable parting of the ways, unless the damage to the property is horrendous, the tenant isn't worth chasing down even if you know where to find the tenant's brother-in-law or where he worked 18 months ago.

I once had a mentally-unstable student who put his head through the walls of the apartment, necessitating all new sheetrock, but fortunately, that was a one-time-only event. There was no way to predict he was unstable, and the university where he attended was able to assist me in getting the repairs paid for, and that's all I could ask for. When the damage was repaired, the apartment was, in effect, brand new, and I kicked the rent $25 per month and rented it to the first looker. The point is that it wasn't worth it to me to chase this young man with all the damage he created; I put my make-ready team into high gear and had the unit back on the market within two days.

Each has to find what works best for him, but one man who had sold me two duplexes and who still owned other rental properties, spent his life at the courthouse chasing deadbeat tenants. His properties were of the low-rent variety, and I doubt that he ever collected a dime from these folks. After watching him file for dollar judgments and reporting to credit companies – most of which turned into animated tail-chasing on his part – I decided it just wasn't worth it. If these people had the money, they would have paid the rent. It was just too easy to clean up a unit that had been trashed. His operation was a self-fulfilling prophecy of "You have to take steps to protect yourself from *them*," and he sure had his fair share of problems.

I found the computerized tracking method which worked best for me and my operation was to use a word processing program and just listed the property address with the name of the tenant and the date the rent was due. I liked collecting rents throughout the month because it evened out my cash flow. I paid my suppliers and contractors when they gave me the bills, and I did not run up charges beyond one month.

Tenants were given a choice when they first rented from me. The rent could run from the date the first rent was paid for a period of 30 days, or they could prorate the rent to any date in the month the tenant chose. However, the proration was added onto the month's rent, not shorted on the front end.

In other words, if the tenant rented his apartment on the 23rd of the month, he could pay the rent on the 23rd of the following month. If, however, the tenant chose to pay the rent on the 5th, then he would pay me from the original rent date, or the 23rd, for one month, to the 23rd of the following month, and then add the number of days from the 23rd to the 5th (based on a 30-day month), so that the rent would be one month's rent plus 12 days, which would bring the rental due date to the 5th of the month following.

You may be tempted to short the rent in order to prorate, but one of my fundamental premises is that the tenant has to have a substantial investment in the property once he has decided to rent it. Just as there are people who look for landlords to pay their utility bills because they have bad credit, there are those who look to move in the middle of the month because they don't have to pay for a full 30 days. They figure that if they prorate the rent from, say, the 17th to the 1st, they don't need much cash.

Also, don't forget that while you require the entire deposit to be paid at the time the property is rented, you will accept half the month's rent now and half in 15 days, which makes the expense more tolerable, and which keeps you in charge with no ambiguities about who is responsible for what. In reality, this is a proration, and it just depends on what you call it, but my way works.

Due to the location of many of the properties I owned, I found myself with a lot of student/roommate situations. In those cases, one tenant would generally speak for the others and I didn't necessarily have all the names. Each roommate could give me an individual check for his share, but I would accept only one envelope from each unit each month. If a roommate moved out, the rent still had to be paid in full or the unit would be in default. Either a new roommate replaced him, or the others had to divvy up the difference between themselves. I shifted the responsibility for record-keeping to the students. It was to the benefit of the roommates that whoever lived there pay his fair share so there were no freeloaders. It was a self-monitoring situation that worked wonderfully well. I never got in the middle of these discussions, but I never had a problem anyway.

I did make it a practice to photocopy checks because in addition to having the address and phone number, I also had the banking information. This came in handy when a check bounced and I had to determine if I could put it back through without it bouncing again. When this happened, I informed the tenant that there was a problem with the check and assumed that it was an innocent error, which the tenant would fix. Usually, the tenant came to me before the check was returned and made good on it. I charged a $20 returned-check fee, which no one ever argued with and most felt was fair.

All of these considerations were taken into account, and I would divide my list by the date the rent was due. As each payment came in, I would line off that tenant with a yellow highlighter. It was easy to tell who had not paid and who was late. It was simple but efficient. Half came in on the first, the rest were spread throughout the month, and some were paid twice a month for the additional $10 service fee.

Chapter 7: Roaches and Other Bugs, or: The High Cost of Tuition in the School of Hard Knocks

How many times have you wished you had someone else's expensive experiences to learn from before you fell into the same financial trap?

Well, here is your opportunity to learn the expensive lessons I learned over many years of landlording. As with most issues of life, particularly those which involve the potential investment of hard cash, a cost-benefit analysis usually dictates which course of action to take when deciding whether to repair or replace.

Here is my cost-benefit analysis in a nutshell: With the exception of the building itself, if it breaks, replace it. Period. It usually isn't worth fiddling around with, especially if it is more than five years old. By the time you apply a quick fix, you will end up repairing it two or three times, and you could have had a new one and forgotten about it. There is only one other consideration. Repairs can be expensed on your tax return while replaced equipment is capitalized on a cash-flow basis. I believe it is a far superior investment to replace.

In addition, if you replace, you don't have to worry about hearing about the item again, usually for many years. Broken repairs, on the other hand, are seldom considerate about timing when they need to be fixed again. And then there is the issue of who is responsible; the repairman can claim that the broken part is one he didn't fix, and so it's not included in his warranty; maybe he guaranteed his work for 90 days and this is the 93rd day. It's not worth the argument to decide who is responsible. If you just replace it, then odds are, it won't break again at all and no one has to be responsible. In addition, no matter what has broken or the reason, you end up paying much more for repairs, including aggravation, than it would have cost to replace it to begin with.

I once met a woman in Abilene who had spent most of her life in Boston. We were discussing dry cleaning for reasons that escape me, but she told me that because dry cleaning in Boston was so expensive, she assumed a dress was good for three wearings before needing to be thrown out. This was a surprising statement, so of course, I asked why. She said a dress she purchased for $100 would cost $30 to dry clean once; by the time she had it cleaned three times, it made more sense to replace it.

I began to apply the same principle to other areas. The most important issue to me was analyzing what it cost to repair a given item once. For example, a new water heater with a minimum warranty costs about $350. Water heaters don't care that it's a Sunday or a holiday when they decide to pop and spew water all over the place. In fact, there is more use of the item on Sunday and holidays because people are home to use them. If you take into account the extra cost of having to fix it on a holiday, it can cost up to $100 to $125 for a plumber and parts and all you have is a repaired water heater with no warranty. When it breaks again – and it will – you've paid for the cost of a new one which won't break again for a long, long time.

When I say *it*, I am referring to everything from water heaters to garage door openers to broken locks to window air conditioners and space heaters. When you price these items, you will find that it's usually not worth your while to pay a higher price for a long-term guarantee, especially something like a water heater. One water heater, with a ten-year guarantee, for example, costs twice the price of one with a minimum guarantee, for exactly the same item. If it were to break within the 10-year warranty period, you'll be shocked to learn that not only is the item depreciated for the amount of time it's been used, but you would have to pay to ship the unit to the manufacturer in order to take advantage of the warranty. It's cheaper to replace the item than it is to go through those gyrations. Besides, what do you do for hot water while it is out being repaired?

There are a couple of caveats to the replace-versus-repair argument. Whatever else you do, make sure that whatever replacement parts you buy are of good quality, especially if that part can cause a lot of damage if it fails. A former landlord of my daughter's updated the bathroom and used the cheapest faucets and toilet he could find. The handle broke off the shower faucet, so her husband jimmy-rigged it with a vise grip until it could be permanently fixed. The bathtub overflow backed up, and the toilet plugged up if the slightest amount of toilet paper were flushed. The end result was a nice hole and a lot of peeling paint in the kitchen ceiling, which was right underneath the bathroom, because of the water damage. The damage was still there when they moved out. You don't have to buy the most expensive, top-of-the-line parts available, but you don't want the bottom-of-the-barrel, either.

The other caveat is that you may have an older building that has built-in amenities that can't be replaced, only repaired. I owned a duplex in Abilene that had a built-in unit in each kitchen that had sink, stove, and oven all in one. Ripping it out and replacing these with modern appliances would have been difficult, but since they were still in good condition, it didn't matter that much and I found a wonderful plumber who could fix anything and tell a good Conway Twitty joke while he did it.

If something breaks, it won't matter if you replace or repair if you don't fix it in a timely manner. The words "I'll get around to it" shouldn't cross your lips, ever. My daughter's landlord learned a very expensive lesson because he kept promising to fix the hole in the kitchen ceiling and paint. Had he a) done the bathroom right to begin with, and b) fixed the ceiling when the damage first became apparent, it would have been a few hours on a Saturday and the cost of some drywall and paint. Instead, it's going to cost a few thousand dollars, if he's lucky.

Unless you're retired with nothing but time on your hands, you're not going to be able to respond to every single request to have something fixed right when the tenant calls. This is where your handy list of service people comes in. Simply call the appropriate provider and make arrangements to have the tenant meet him. If you can, have a three-way conference call with you, the tenant, and the service provider so the tenant can describe the problem and make arrangements for the service call and you can authorize the repair.

An understandable concern of tenants is pest control, and there are many different ways to approach it. Some tenants won't move into an apartment unless there is monthly pest control service, but in truth, I have discovered that this is the most ineffective way to approach the problem unless you are the pest control service.

I made a study of the life cycle of the common house roach, the most prevalent pest there is, besides mice. If left uncontrolled, roaches will become a nightmare whose only solution seems to be burning the building down. Before I learned how to control the problem, actually, an actual fire was the only way we were able to get rid of it.

Roaches usually make their way into an apartment when tenants bring them in from the market in shopping bags, and it is unintentional. If a tenant had a roach problem in his old apartment, some roaches will come over intact, no matter how carefully he packed.

Most people don't know this, but the cockroach goes back to prehistoric times, and look who is still here. One time, I had an infestation in my kitchen pantry when we decided to move into a temporary residence while our house was being completed. Not wanting to take any additional "pets" with us, I carefully washed and packed each and every dish, can of food, clothing, bedding, anything that could be washed and sterilized in the dishwasher, and then carefully packed everything into sturdy cardboard moving cartons, knowing that everything would be stored for an indeterminate amount of time in the unfinished living room.

I still believed in the idea of "who's bigger, me or the roach?" It had become me or them. A year passed before our renovated home was ready for us to move into. To my horror, when I unpacked the boxes, and without anything edible anywhere around, I discovered live roaches in the boxes I had packed so carefully *a year before*. I became a believer that roaches could outlive *anything*.

I discovered that the life cycle of the roach is ten days from birth to sexual maturity. They are hatched from eggs, which poisons cannot penetrate. Roach control products kill live roaches in various states of maturity, but it seems that the last thing a sprayed female does before she dies is to drop her eggs. We know that once the eggs are passed from the female, there is a ten-day time frame until these newly-hatched roaches will mature and drop their own eggs. Therefore, to spray for roaches every month is pointless because there is enough time for three generations of roaches to hatch and reproduce, literally tens of thousands of them. That's why monthly service will always be needed.

However, if you spray on, say, the 1st of the month, and then again on the 10th, you will get the mature ones and the "teenagers", but if you assume that impenetrable eggs have been laid on the 1st, there will be hatchlings by the 10th, which, because they are now live roaches and not eggs, will die off in the second go-around. Usually, this is enough to stop the problem, but if you aren't sure, then a third spraying ten days after that will cure the problem entirely. You shouldn't have any more problems until a tenant brings them in from the outside.

If there are multiple units at a given location which share common walls and attics, you need to do all of the units at the same time for obvious reasons. The roaches who can will migrate to the untreated unit, there to proliferate even worse. Operation Annihilation requires unwavering determination on the part of everyone who has to take part, but the results are worth it.

I found that roach control products carried at farm-supply stores seem to be more effective than those bought, for example, at the supermarket. Raid, Roach Motel, and other such products may work for some, but I have not had success with them. Actually, I found the product that works best is Bengal. It is difficult to find, more expensive than most, but it is worth the hunt. I have only found it in farm-supply stores, but some hardware stores and supermarkets carry it, or you can order it from www.bengal.com.

To continue with the Tale of the Roach, these products kill live roaches, not eggs, usually regardless of what the can might say. In the quintessential tradition of survival of the fittest (or most tenacious), the last thing a dying mother roach does is lay her eggs before she whales over, gasping her last breath. Also, keep in mind that there are literally thousands of roaches in the walls and attic, as well, which don't come out in the light.

These critters lay thousands of eggs at a time, so diligence in the treatment schedule not only pays off in as total a destruction of the problem as possible over long periods of time, but if you waver in completing it, you have to start over again because new generations are being brought along in the absence of your attention.

If you prefer a professional exterminator to handle the job, then arrange a convenient time when all the tenants in the building can participate by emptying the property of people, pets, and items from cupboards, and be sure to advise the tenants to wash all items thoroughly before putting them away. In order to be the most effective, however, be sure that the re-spray is in not in 30 days, but in 10 days, then 10 days after that, if necessary.

Often, tenants are embarrassed to complain about roaches and try to exterminate them themselves. Be sure to assure the tenants that if a problem develops, that you need to be notified before it gets out of hand, so that all tenants can have their homes treated with a minimum of inconvenience. If you are matter-of-fact, the tenant will be the same. The same approach is necessary for all vermin or pests, regardless of species.

In addition to making your property look presentable, keeping the yard cleaned up will help keep pest problems to a minimum. Snakes, venomous spiders, and scorpions like to hide in dark places, such as woodpiles, stacks of debris, and tall grass. Mosquitoes lay eggs in standing water. Depending on where you live, you may have other pests you don't want invading your property, such as rats. Keeping the yard clear and standing water drained will remove any potential homes for these creatures and the food that attracts them. It will also keep your municipality off your back. One final comment is that keeping a clear yard will also remove those things that may be an attractive nuisance to children. No one wants to see a child hurt (or worse) because of something that could have been prevented.

There is one problem landlords share with a cross section of our society, from which no one is exempt: drugs. Under both federal and state laws, landlords can be put in a position of having to forfeit their property if it is discovered that there is drug use on the property, regardless of whether the landlord has any idea that drug use or possession is on the premises. "Not seeing" that there is a drug problem does not get you off the hook, but there are things which you can do to protect yourself, and which will give you a defense should you risk loss of your property under seizure laws.

Pay attention to any unusually busy activity. Remember, you are renting residential property, not space in a shopping mall. Except for birthday parties and Christmas, there should not be much coming and going on a regular basis. No one is that popular, particularly if the comings and goings are for short periods. Sometimes it is difficult to be able to be at the property enough to notice this. I usually paid attention when I was at a particular apartment making it ready for a new tenant, or when I was doing yard work or something that would allow me to be present at the property for a day or two.

Drug dealers, not wanting to attract a lot of attention, usually pay the rent in cash and on time, so as not to attract attention, though this is, by no means, exclusive to the criminal element. When there is a lot of activity, coupled with those paying habits, I notified the local police that I am the owner of the property at that address, that I rented the property to a particular tenant, and that I suspect drug use and/or possession with intent to sell going on at the property. I make sure that the police enter the call on their blotter so that there is a record of the report.

I hate to be the one to point out the obvious, and by no means, does this apply to all police departments everywhere, but drug use and the crimes involved are so commonplace today that even police departments don't seem to get that excited about it. The usual response to my call reporting my suspicions was something like there was not probable cause to search the premises, and once, (I still can't believe this one), "we don't have the resources to send out a cruiser."

Based upon calls I had received from tenants and neighbors, I reported a tenant for dealing drugs. He was on parole for drug distribution, and the local police responded by saying that they lacked the resources to do anything about it. This desk sergeant also informed me that it was not the local police who were monitoring this fellow, but the state police. It wasn't a local problem.

My concern, aside from the well-being and safety of my tenants and others who might be on my property, was also for my ownership of the property, something the local police didn't want to hear. However, I was so appalled at this response that I was motivated to call the mayor's office, where I did get action in a hurry.

The tenant was apprehended, tried and sent to prison for life as a result of my tenacity, and it proved to be the biggest drug bust in the history of the community! And, not only did I not face the loss of my property, but I learned that it is important to go through the motions of disclosure first.

When I went through those gyrations, which I had to do from time to time, I always told the tenant I suspected of dealing what my suspicions were, what they were based on, and that I had reported it to the police. I would just tell them that they had an awful lot of friends visiting during a week-day when they should have been at work. So, not only did I suspect their "friends" were coming to either buy or deliver drugs, but that they didn't have any other means of support.

It is important to understand that I am not the police, do not have the authority (nor do I want it), to make an arrest, but I can sure report what I suspect. I invited the tenant to reach his own conclusions, and to act accordingly. I did not take these actions lightly. However, if the tenant was so engaged, then you can be sure that he would be gone by morning, saving me the trouble of having to prove drug use in court in an eviction proceeding. I guess my instincts were right on, because I never had anyone challenge my suspicions.

Forfeiture and seizure laws do not just apply to drug use, however, but extend to any crimes in which the property (not just real estate, either) may have been involved, or which could have been purchased with ill-gotten gains. Most landlords find it not in their best interest to put up with criminal activity on moral grounds.

The landlord needs to be aware that the most innocent of us have been unwittingly put into compromising situations resulting in the forfeiture of everything we've worked for. The moral is that you can't be too careful and decide that it's better to feel silly and safe than silly and sorry.

Chapter 8: Hunting for Tenants and Keeping Them Happy

Not everyone is meant to be a landlord, just as not everyone is meant to knit or fix cars (or even be a tenant). However, owning real property for the purpose of making homes available for others can be rewarding, and, if you are willing to embellish your repair and decorating skills, can be quite lucrative.

You need to do as much of the work in caring for your properties as you can. When, for example, a tenant reports to you that he got an extraordinary water bill, you can be assured that the tenant is suffering from either a leaky faucet or a running toilet. If you had to hire a plumber each time you needed to replace a three-dollar ballcock, your profits will, literally, go down the toilet. It's too easy to learn yourself, with help from the local hardware store and a little time spent on YouTube.

Often, hardware superstores, like Home Depot, Builder's Square, Lowe's and many others, offer classes in how to do everything wallpapering a bathroom to how to install closet poles, hook up washers and dryers as well as plumbing, simple electrical (and when to know when you are in over your head) and carpentry repairs.

You should keep a roster of contractors who are willing to make their services available to you because you can certainly promise volumes of work to make it worth their while. I found a wonderful plumber who made himself available for the oddest of plumbing posers at the oddest of hours, and for a very reasonable sum. I also found a handyman who loved challenges and always rose to the occasion, fixing everything from inset doors to fashioning sheet metal to create a vent for a water heater and fixed leaky roofs. Their work was excellent, seldom had to be redone, which made me, as the one who was able to send them out almost on command, look very, very good. Also, there was a wonderful pride of workmanship in all of these folks, and when I had to ask them to redo something, or re-check work they had done for me, it was taken care of.

Because they were working on such a low profit margin, I preferred to pay them upon receipt of invoice, making almost my entire operation a cash-and-carry business. Because I structured my rental incomes from tenants so that they came in throughout the month, I always had sufficient cash on hand to be able to keep up with it, making my year-end accountings a breeze for my accountant.

I also found that it was prudent to hire out yardwork. I had so many lawns to mow, from little squares to places which looked like parks, I was able to find people who would work for a flat rate per lawn, making it up on smaller ones to compensate for the larger ones, although it was probably more trouble to unload the equipment for the smaller jobs.

Once a year I negotiated with the lawn people to trim the trees and stack the wood so that people going through the back alleys would have something to take. I was spared the cost to haul it off and there were people who could use it for firewood.

I already detailed why it is not good practice to arrange a trade-off with tenants for lawn mowing services; however, having the buildings look tidy at all times was very important to me. Not only did my properties have great street appeal, but the tenants could rely on their having a place where they were proud to bring visitors. It was a morale thing, but extremely important.

If tenants wanted to plant flowers or vegetables, I invited it, which, of course, the tenants tended. Many really appreciated the opportunity of having a place to indulge in "dirt therapy," a benefit not usually enjoyed by apartment dwellers. At one location, a tenant was a student majoring in horticulture. She organized all of the tenants to grow a huge vegetable garden. When all the tenants who are interested in participating have moved on, it is a simple matter of a little soil amendment and some sod to fill in the garden. It is worth the cost, however, in satisfied tenants who do not move too often.

As a small operator you can afford to be more friendly toward tenants, and you can offer them extras, like agreeing to their gardening or decorating. It is important that your tenants see you in a different, more amiable light than they get in large complexes where they get an apartment and a parking space. In those circumstances, hired employees are responsible for taking care of the tenants' needs. The same is true if you engage the services of a management company.

I think back to the times when I was a renter, and how demeaning the process of attempting to find a home was. I guess I am too paranoid, or too insecure, and always felt like I wasn't good enough, no matter how fast I managed to tap dance for the manager. Further, I didn't appreciate someone prying into my personal life, wanting to make me personally responsible if the crystal ball of the future fogged up and the bottom fell out of the economy.

I was reminded of that demeaning experience when my son moved to a major city to attend law school. He attempted to rent an apartment, and, though he was an adult who offered to pre-pay six months' rent to the management company, they, nonetheless, required my tax returns. I refused to be contractually bound, but they still insisted upon seeing proof of ownership of my home and my credit report. To show how ridiculous this is, the most they stood to lose if my son defaulted on his agreement with them was $300, which they already had in the form of a deposit. When I discovered that other parents put the skids on these outrageous requests, I felt somewhat mollified.

My point in these anecdotes is that by putting myself in the place of my tenants through recollections, I believe that the method I use to qualify tenants not only protects me from tenants I'd rather not have to deal with, but also allows me to extend a courtesy to my tenants that renting an apartment is not a lifetime commitment with promises of perpetual perfection in credit relations.

How to Write Ads Which Attract and Screen at the Same Time

You don't need a degree in copywriting to put together an ad which will attract the tenants you want. Remember that you are appealing to a different market from that of a large complex. Your ads should reflect a friendlier lack of forbidding formality and it is your ad which dictates how much rent to charge for your properties. If you have to show a particular property more than three times, you are charging too much, period. It does not matter what other landlords are getting for rent in other buildings in other neighborhoods (or even in your neighborhood). All that matters is what you can rent your property for. If you have gotten a certain rent before and are not able to attract that much now, you need to take a closer look at the property to see if it still commands the price you are asking. Maybe there is an unpleasant odor that you didn't notice, but others do. If that is the case, then maybe the carpet needs shampooing or changing, for example.

It is better to correct the problems with the unit and get the price you want than to reduce the price with the property in a lesser condition, which is reviewed in Chapter 3. If a property does not rent by the third showing, I have found it very helpful to just ask the prospect what he is not real impressed with. Few prospects will come right out and voluntarily tell you that they just don't like the place, but if you ask they are glad to share with you. Thank the prospect for his honesty, but forget him as a tenant; fix the problems he outlined and try again. Sometimes the prospect will offer to take the property at a reduced price in the condition you have discussed. Thank the prospect again and decline the offer.

It is always better if you can raise the rent for new tenants each time you turn the unit over. Of course, this depends upon the housing market in general, but if the prior tenants have fixed the place up, and if you've done a fine job of making it ready, you should be able to raise the rents incrementally until all the units in the building are at the same level, then raise it again. For example, if you start off at renting four units in a building at $300 per month, the property is maintained, then you should be able to raise the rent to $325 once the first of the four tenants moves out. When the second moves out, re-rent that one at $325 also, and so forth, until all four are renting to no more than the third prospect, or $325; when the second round comes up, you should be able to easily rent it for $350, and so forth. Not only should your costs remain relatively fixed so that these increases go to your bottom line, but it adds value to the property since value is computed as a multiple of the rental income.

I always had good luck with classified ads in the daily newspapers, but many cities no longer have a newspaper that prints daily. They do, however, have websites that accept for-rent ads. Again, don't list the address of the property, and use good photos that show the unit's best features. Craig's List is another good option in many cities, as is apartments.com. You can also find contractors and service providers through these sites, as well.

Facebook and Twitter can be effective places to advertise, as well. You can list individual units (without the address, of course), and people can share, re-tweet, and help spread the word about your properties. If you decide to go the sponsored post route, your ads can be targeted to specific people, and they're not too expensive. You might also talk to the people at your local newspaper about advertising on their website, which is also inexpensive.

If you live in a college or military town, and you want to reach those markets, find out what the newspaper is called and call to place an ad. If the college has a radio station, find out about advertising there, as well. These are fairly reasonable, price-wise, and you will reach a different market.

No matter what you, the adage about not putting all your eggs in one basket holds true. There are a lot of different places to advertise what you have to offer, but don't concentrate all on Internet or print or radio. Put a good marketing plan together and follow it.

The best response came from ads which highlighted a feature of the unit I was renting, which I did not place until the apartment was completely ready for occupancy. I always began the ad with the number of bedrooms, always included the price and the deposit at the end of the ad before the phone number, and made sure to mention if the unit had washer/dryer hookups or had a good-sized yard. If it was near a university campus, I advertised that the tenant could walk to campus.

The way the ad is worded limits from whom you may expect to receive phone calls. A family of four, for example, is not going to respond to an ad for a one-bedroom apartment (if someone does, it is a screaming red flag, and even if that family is willing to compromise, you just cite health- or fire-code violations!)

Be prepared for animal lovers to respond to ads promoting large, fenced yards. I never had a problem renting to people with pets, though I frowned on those who assured me that the dog stayed outside. To me, that is not a pet, and it is obviously not housebroken. I would try to avoid moralizing about people who keep animals in such circumstances, and sometimes other tenants in the same complex, having seen one tenant with a pet, will help themselves to one of their own.

The only time I would compromise making a deal with a tenant was in the case of carpeting that really needed to be changed; if he agreed to take the house with the existing carpet then I would waive a pet deposit, reasoning that I would just change the carpet when this tenant moved out. Sometimes it worked so well that I never changed the carpet in some units.

In the situations where carpeting was not an issue, I would take a $200 to $300 *non-refundable* pet deposit, which people were glad to pay. Under no circumstances would I ever consent to rent to tenants with pit bull terriers (a popular breed in the southern United States), or to those with Rottweilers. The liability a landlord might incur in the event these particular breeds of dog entered an altercation could be potentially devastating, and just wasn't worth it. Sometimes you have to deal with a "love me, love my dog" mentality, but you really can't afford to give in on this issue.

In the event that you provide appliances, and it is standard in your community, you really can't add for those items. In fact, in the few instances when tenants have asked if I could remove appliances (particularly refrigerators), I would have to tell them that there would be a $40 charge because I would have to pay someone $20 to take it out and $20 to bring it back, but I would cheerfully offer to do it.

The final and ultimate qualifier in your ad is the price. Prospective tenants tend to turn to the section with the price range they have in mind for housing, and which they can afford. If you are advertising a 2-bedroom duplex with a large, fenced yard, washer/dryer connections, stove and refrigerator for $325 per month with a deposit of $175, you are not renting the Taj Mahal, the prospect knows that, and doesn't expect it.

By the same token, if you are advertising a single family residence for $1725 per month, you can expect a nice family neighborhood, good schools, all the amenities such a house in such a neighborhood would command, but it's not Beverly Hills. Here is where your attention to condition comes in—if it rents within the first three showings, then you know that the property is as advertised, and is a good value for the price.

Never exaggerate what you have to offer. During the time when you are first meeting your prospective tenants, first impressions are everything. Not only is the tenant interested in paying you money for a pleasant place to live at a price he can afford and he is entrusting you with their safety and well-being; he is entrusting your common sense and good judgment about the character and trustworthiness of workpeople whom you may need to hire to enter his property when he isn't home.

You need to be neatly attired (you don't have to overdo, clean jeans is okay, too), but make sure your car is presentable and reasonably clean, and that you have the correct keys. I sold a building in a university community to a young man who favored torn tee shirts, sported a ponytail, and enjoyed rebuilding wrecked (and I do mean wrecked) cars as a sideline. I raise this anecdote to illustrate that, while the car may ultimately bring a king's ransom when he restores it, nonetheless, it hardly inspires confidence in college students and their parents, particularly with safety issues.

Since the young man had incurred a 20-year obligation to me for the purchase of the building, I felt compelled to point out a more appropriate approach to inspiring confidence in prospective tenants. Fortunately, his partner (his mother) and he listened, and they have become a real success story.

You can assume, through selective advertising, that anyone who answers the ad and is motivated to make an appointment to see it, should be likely to want to rent it. The cardinal rule is "show, don't tell". Don't try to sell the apartment over the phone because the prospect has no visual reference. Just make the appointment and let the place speak for itself. If the tenant likes it, he will rent it. If you sell it over the phone, the tenant may decide you're being too pushy, or that there's something wrong with it and take his business elsewhere.

If you show it, but the prospects go to look at another apartment because he feels honor-bound to see it, odds are you won't see these folks again. If they indicate that they like yours and ask you to hold it, do not do so without a deposit with a short time limit. The more time that goes by without your hearing back, the less likely you are to refund any of the deposit because you are in the rental business, not the property-holding-to-accommodate-apartment-shopping business, and time is money.

Never tell this prospect that you have other appointments to show the unit unless you do, and make sure to make it clear that you are not telling the prospect this to pressure him into a decision, but you feel it is only fair to let them know the status. Don't take a deposit to hold an apartment for comparison purposes if you have other appointments to show it. If the property is still available, you would be happy to rent it to him if he is still interested.

As a landlord, state and federal discrimination laws restrict your choices of tenants in many areas. Obviously, it is illegal to discriminate on the basis of race or religion. I had rented one unit to a young lady who happened to be pregnant. Apparently, her husband, about whom I did not feel it was my business to ask, worked out of town, so I did not have occasion to meet him until much later; suffice it to say that she gave birth about the time we had decided to sell the buildings. I took one prospective buyer through the building. He saw the young woman with the baby and had the audacity to ask whether she was married. I explained to him, in no uncertain terms, that not only did it never occur to me to be ill-bred enough to ask, but that if it was none of my business, it certainly wasn't any of his. We opted to sell the building to someone else. You *can* discriminate in the sale of income property. You cannot inquire into someone's sexual orientation, nor into any other aspect of his lifestyle. As long as the tenants are respectful of their neighbors, pay the rent on time and report problems to me, I have not one whit of interest in anything else about their personal lives, nor should you. If you feel a moral obligation to discriminate against *anyone*, you should reconsider managing rental income property. Obviously you have a right to be concerned about criminal activity on your property, but beyond that, commentary about anything else is *verboten.*

Raising rents on existing tenants was a practice I came to avoid after one experience. I realized, after reviewing my records, that four tenants had lived in their apartments for more than a year. I decided that a rent-raise of $10 was not out of line, and informed these great folks about the increase. Two decided to move out. These folks had been wonderful tenants, and I decided that a fifty percent loss rate wasn't worth it. From that point on, I only increased rents when the tenants moved out.

I have always encouraged tenants to express themselves by decorating their spaces, and I've been lucky enough to rent to some very talented people, often to college students who proved to be art majors. Not one to disparage true artistic expression, not only did I allow tenants to improve their spaces, but did not change or charge them for expressing their true selves, which less talented tenants to follow did have the good sense to appreciate, and at a premium in the rent. Often, these tenants had their own replacements lined up in the wings.

In those units where I was not so lucky in the artistic area, I discovered the wallpaper store discontinued bin. For a dollar or two, I was able to buy several rolls of wallpaper borders, which I used to accent rooms in units. It was amazing how much more rent I was able to charge for these small improvements, because they were unexpected and they served to cheer the units up considerably. I also found it helpful to paint all apartments the same color; this made buying paint much easier; also, if you need to touch up a few spots, you can do that without re-painting the entire apartment. Before I learned this lesson, I bought several gallons of mis-mixed paint to re-paint an apartment. I figured the paint was such a bargain, the color didn't matter. Much to my surprise (and dismay), I opened the first can to find Pepto-Bismol pink. After that, I stuck with a more neutral shade. Of course, if the tenant wants a different color, he is more than welcome to paint the apartment himself.

The final step in successful renting is to always hold something back from your promotions and ads. Often, prospective tenants have formed a visual image which is of interest on its own or he would not make an appointment to see the property in person. But, if when the prospect comes to the property and the lawn is neatly trimmed, with bushes neatly trimmed, and you are there waiting, it can only get better. When you open the door to a pleasant-smelling, clean and cheerful place, the prospect can only be impressed from that point on. I have heard more prospects (and, usually, tenants) complain about the quality of properties they have looked at compared to mine, that it is a point of pride that I feel confident that there are few tenants to whom I have rented who would not write me a letter of recommendation if I asked. That's about the best it gets!

Chapter 9: Know Thy Rules

While I am firmly convinced that in most communities around the country, common sense prevails for the most part, but it's to your benefit to learn about local laws that may affect your ownership of your property. You also need to know what you are required to do to protect the health and safety of your tenants and your own liability.

You need to pay particular attention to issues like security, lighting, animals owned by your tenants, and attractive nuisances which could be interesting to not only children of your tenants, but to others as well. This includes others who may be enticed to enter your property whether or not anyone knows he's there.

You also need to discuss your liability insurance with a good commercial insurance agent. This person can tell you want you need and what you don't. You will certainly need a policy to cover the physical dwelling, and you will also want to discuss liability and business insurance policies. You do need to make it clear to your tenants, however, that your insurance does not cover their personal belongings, and that they need to carry renter's insurance that does. Renter's insurance is fairly cheap and can be purchased from their auto carrier.

The issue you will have to deal with most often, especially if you have a number of units, is the issue of knowing the steps you will need to ask a tenant to leave for non-payment of rent. Usually, this is the easiest to solve because the issues are clear-cut: Either the rent was paid, or it wasn't.

In order for a tenant to use the defense that he offset expenses against the rent due, he had to have followed a prescribed list of requirements, the last option of which was to pay for repairs, or equipment, or whatever, and to deduct it from the rent. It could not be done arbitrarily or by whimsy. Laws usually set this down.

The tenant is first required to notify the landlord in writing that there is a problem, and specify what the problem is, and when it would be convenient for the landlord to access the apartment to repair it. The landlord is given a specified number of days to make repairs, taking into consideration weather, strikes, and other things outside his control, but reasonable attempts are considered. This especially includes if the tenant somehow interferes with the landlord's ability to access the property.

If the tenant notifies the landlord in writing and the repairs are not done, then the tenant may hire someone to make the repairs, and, attaching the paid receipt to the reduced rent check, offset the repairs. Without this specific exception, unless the landlord specifically gives authorization in writing, the tenant may not engage the services of another and expect the landlord to pay for it. Of course, common sense dictates that if there is an immediate danger and the landlord can't be contacted, the tenant should take action to fix the problem.

If the cost of the repairs exceeds the amount of the rent, for example, there are other remedies available to the tenant, such as a constructive eviction, including reimbursement for emergency lodging (if there is, for example, a fire making the property unlivable).

If, after all best efforts, the problem still is not, or cannot be fixed, then the tenant and landlord need to come to some arrangement as to what compensation will be given for the inconvenience. If the problem is that extensive or that expensive, you should probably file an insurance claim; the cost of the deductible is probably going to be a lot lower than paying to fix the damage yourself.

If the property is not habitable, then the agreement may be voidable, necessitating the tenant's moving out, whether the tenant is responsible or not. A wise landlord would inconvenience the tenant as little as possible, would analyze the cost to himself for various resolutions, and pick the least expensive, least intrusive and disruptive way out of the situation. A tenant suing a landlord for a problem such as this could result in astronomical damages against the landlord, and the worst decision that a landlord can make is to ignore the problem.

A fair question is whether or not to list your available properties with HUD and/or other agencies which supplement or pay rent for prospective tenants (their "clients") who meet certain financial and other criteria. Having made certain properties available for this market, and having jumped through the hoops required to do so, I concluded that these programs were not for me.

In these situations, there are three parties to the contract (which has to be contained within one, multi-page document). As the landlord, you are pitted against the interests of the tenant and of the government, forming a three-way tug-of-war. While I had pretty high standards of my own, those of the government were often outlandish. There are advantages, and local HUD authorities work with landlords, offering a lot of advice. I used to attend HUD meetings for landlords, and found that the primary focus of the agenda was "How to Protect Ourselves from Them."

I had long ago determined that I needed "*Them*" because "*they*" provide my livelihood, which led directly to my desire to experiment with other methods of dealing and working with tenants which was not so adversarial, the results of which I have tried to outline here.

The consequences of having three entities as separate parties to this three-way contract was that contained within that document were requirements of the government which I, as an individual, did not have and, frankly, found objectionable. For example, it made no difference to me whether the tenant had guests staying within the property without my consent (usually they told me about it), but the government required the landlord to conduct a head count to ensure that only those listed by name within the contract be inside the residence.

My biggest objection to renting under a government-sponsored rental supplemental program arose after the tenants vacated the property. While the governmental agency offers reimbursement for damages done to the property by tenants, collecting the money is a different matter.

The terms of the contract require that the repairs be made and the claim be presented within 30 days after the tenant vacates the premises. In the only instance when I found it necessary to present a claim, the tenants had moved out on the first of December, meaning that the repairs (which were considerable), had to be assessed and completed throughout the Christmas and New Year holidays, the time of year when it is virtually impossible to find workmen to do the repairs. I did the best I could do under the circumstances and had the claim ready to file on January 3, but it was rejected as having been filed outside the deadline.

The damages totaled more than $1,500 and when I calmed down long enough after the claim was rejected, I discovered that all the reimbursement I could have collected under the particular program this family was a part of, was $50. Talk about a cost/benefit analysis, this was not effective!

It was also this particular situation which taught me to collect the deposit up front even if it meant that I had to accept the rent being paid out. This fellow gave me $50 of a $150 deposit, always promised the rest sometime in the future, but it somehow never showed up. So, I didn't even get the deposit money out of the deal. Live and learn, and how!

In all fairness, there have been changes for the better. At the time I participated in the HUD program, the directors of the program could not disclose to potential landlords the fact that tenants left former rentals in shambles, for example, and under the law, the agency was not allowed to pass that on. One of the "Protect Yourself from Them" tips was to be sure that you called and spoke with former landlords, who could issue reports on the condition in which properties had been left.

What was particularly annoying was that these folks were still allowed to participate in rent subsidy programs. This has changed. If a property is left in a trashed condition and the vacating tenant does not make arrangements to compensate for the damage, he is summarily dismissed from the subsidy rolls and another family is quickly substituted. The tenant has to make restitution and cannot be restored until the damages have been paid for. This turns into a self-regulating situation because individuals who have been deleted from the program for cause will not be referred to you for housing.

Since these changes, I probably would consider giving the program another try and, in all fairness, HUD is interested in attracting landlords with well-maintained properties and is willing to pay a premium rent to compensate. Also, once the property has passed the initial inspection, renewal is usually, with little exception, automatic provided the property is kept in excellent condition.

Consistency in dealing with your tenants is the best favor you can do for yourself. It is in your best interest to live up to promises made to the tenants at the time he decided to rent from you, whether stated or implied. For example, if you are lucky enough to get a heads-up about a problem needing attention, it is important that you tend to it voluntarily and preemptively. Not only does this prevent a potentially damaging situation, but it gives the tenants a sense of well-being, which goes to the longevity of his tenancy, the ongoing care of the property, and all the issues of concern to both landlord and tenant.

Certain precautions are advisable even though it may not yet be law in your jurisdiction. For example, Texas now requires that landlords provide not only traditional deadbolts (the shorter one is legal, but the longer one is preferable), but also requires a "blind" dead bolt, which is invisible from the exterior, but which can be locked from the inside when the tenant is home. These devices prevent anyone from using a key to gain entrance when the tenant is home. If your community does not yet have this requirement, you should take the initiative to install them anyway.

Locks always need to be re-keyed each time a tenant vacates. There are several ways to accomplish this. I always keyed multiple doors in a given unit to the same key so that there were not a lot of keys floating around. I provided one key to the tenant at the time he moved in. If the tenant wanted more than one key, he would have to duplicate mine. I kept possession of all duplicate keys, not giving them out to the people who worked for me except if the unit was vacant. I always preferred that the tenants be home; if he felt insecure about having workmen in the apartment when he was alone, then he could arrange for a friend to be there.

I kept a spare set of locks (keyed the same), so that when a tenant moved out, all I had to do was pull the old locks and substitute them with my spare set, which I replaced with the locks I had just pulled. This way, I always had my own duplicate key which I could copy for a new tenant. If the former tenant took the key(s) with him, it didn't matter because I didn't need them anyway. I also did not charge for key deposits because I felt it created more paperwork and wasn't worth the effort.

If the tenant could not arrange to meet the repairman then I would, but I always was uncomfortable letting even people with whom I had been working for years, enter an apartment unaccompanied for their own protection. It is automatic for police and insurance companies to look toward workmen and repair people who have been inside the premises when items come up missing. If the workman is not left alone, he can't be blamed.

You should discuss security lighting with your local electricity provider. In certain situations, the city or the electric company will provide them; sometimes the landlord has to pay for them, which can be passed through when calculating rent. In most circumstances, the cost is minimal on a monthly basis and should be compared to the cost of a liability claim or injury to a person which could have (and should have) been prevented.

It would be worth your while to engage the services of an attorney specializing in landlord/tenant law for the purpose of providing you with a check list of steps you need to take in order to evict someone for non-payment of rent. You might feel more comfortable using the services of an attorney the first time or two. It is a terrifying prospect, but, if you learn what "t's" to cross and "i's" to dot, it is not difficult to do this for yourself. Like most things in life, there is a formula to learn and follow. After going to court a few times in your own behalf, it becomes easier. You need to be aware that if your business enterprise is incorporated, state law may require a licensed attorney to represent the corporation.

I found that the only interest I had in evicting a tenant was to regain legal possession of the property. Usually, if the tenant had the money to pay the rent, he would have, and often you end up chasing your tail and collecting nothing but a lot of bills to show for it. Finding yourself in a position of having to evict a tenant for reasons other than non-payment of rent may require, at least, consultation with an attorney.

In some jurisdictions, you are able to combine an eviction proceeding with a suit for damages. In others, they are required to be filed as separate actions. In the first, you are usually entitled to possession of the property and the unpaid rent, but not damages for the broken windows or cracked floor tiles. That has to be brought in a separate action, which may not be worth it. After you have had an opportunity to assess the pros and cons by writing them down, you will be able to determine whether the cost is justified. My own experience says that it seldom is but that you should not be 80 afraid to go forward if the damage to your property is over and above an acceptable limit, especially if a third party can assist you in collecting the judgment, or will pay for it.

It is important to keep in mind, however, that the priority is to restore the rental property to a rentable condition even if it means that you have to take a loss on recovering money from the errant previous tenant. Consistent rental production will allow you to recapture the losses much more quickly. A side benefit won't be appreciated until tax time, but these losses can usually be written off, both philosophically and realistically.

Photographs of the damage to the property, including stills and video, will allow you to establish proof in court. Make sure you date and time-stamp the images and download them onto your computer as soon as possible. In fact, each time you rent an apartment, take before-and-after photos so there is a basis for comparison in the event the tenant challenges you on the condition of the apartment when he moved in. Set up a folder for each tenant and keep both sets in that folder. You can also use this folder to keep accounts and other documents for that tenant and it will help you get and stay organized.

In every jurisdiction in the land, there are volumes of laws and cases regulating relationships between landlords and tenants, and these differ as much as there are jurisdictions. While the information contained herein is meant to be a general guideline and is not offered as legal advice, it may be prudent to run these ideas past an attorney.

One last thing I learned is not to deal with more than five or six units in any given location, for several reasons. First, anything more than that will require on-site management. One advantage to Practical Landlording is that you don't need to rely on such help. Often, they find themselves in the middle of a battlefield due to the nature of tenants being what it is. If one is a pain, several will move rather than complain. They tend to form something akin to a union and will often strike. Bad feelings can fester and you will be the bad guy no matter what you do because management will be in the position to take sides one way or the other. You are a small operator and can't afford highly charged emotions. Your on-site management might be the ones to have to go.

Another reason, believe it or not, is that true love may bloom. Say a single man meets the single woman next door. They fall in love and marry. One moves into the unit of the other, leaving you with one empty. Then they fall out of love, both of them hate each other, and they both move out, leaving you with two vacancies. Imagine this multiplied times twenty.

Chapter 10: The Next Level, or: Where do I go from here?

Having spent the last few years in the big city, after using Abilene as a sort of laboratory to try out all my theories and paring them down to what works, I found that I missed landlording a lot. San Antonio is much too large a city to manage properties myself. It would have meant buying buildings I wasn't sure of from a construction standpoint, and the costs of acquisition would be a lot higher. After looking around for about two years, I found that to be the case. I felt I needed to change the focus of my program and so, instead of looking at bigger buildings closer to home, I decided to violate one of my own rules, sort of.

I found a tract builder who was off the beaten track, kind of like me, who purchased odd pieces of land, built no more than 50 or so homes in the community. These houses were from 1100 to 2000 square feet and priced well below the market because of the unusual locations he builds in. I purchased some of these houses, priced the rent at twice the cost of principal and interest, less taxes and insurance, and found that after my successes in Abilene, I could buy them with bank loans. How about that?

So far, I've purchased six of these brand-new houses and lo and behold! My theories outlined in this book work just the same as with apartment and duplex rentals. I use the same guidelines, offer the same perks, rent to pets, offer short-term rentals with no strings attached, just a 30-day notice. I am proud to say, "I knew it, I knew it, I knew it!"

Another surprise hit me unaware that changed my direction, as well – diagnosed with multiple sclerosis in 1996, I found that I am getting worse; I discovered that instead of being able to tend to older properties that took more work, if I bought brand-new houses, with warranties where the builder is responsible for repairs, then I eliminated the need to travel there myself a lot, and the checks come in once a month with not much effort on my part.

In addition, the tenants I am attracting now are people who have usually owned homes before, know what demands are present with living in them, and are between home ownership for some reason. My tenants now are people who have to move out of their homes because of fire, mild, have sold their house and are building another, and the like. In fact, I find that I receive more calls from men than women, that they are not shy about paying more for getting more. One fellow even re-landscaped half an acre while renting. Do I love that!

I advertise the same, promote the same, everything is the same. When the houses are closed at the title company and I own them, I install sprinklers, which are set to water the lawn three times a week, mowed every ten days, have garage-door openers, and homeowner's associations, for which I pay. As a rule, I find that folks who rent a whole brand-new house are squeamish to let anything happen to "someone else's house". I also discovered that there is a huge market for quality rental housing with pets, and that folks who are used to a certain lifestyle should not have to compromise because they find themselves without their home for whatever reason.

In addition to advertising in the daily newspaper, I place ads on Yahoo.com, rent.com, and put my name with insurance companies who often have to pay to put their policy holders up for a while as they are processing claims and re-building. These are great tenants – the insurance company pays the rent, it always shows up on time, and it tends to go on for longer than originally anticipated. Home repair services will also recommend my properties to their clients. The only problem I have had here is having enough product to go around.

APPENDIX Notice to Pay Rent or Quit

This will serve notice upon you that your rent of $____ _____ is now past due and you are in default of our agreement, dated _____(date of signed

receipt). You must pay all back owed amounts, totaling $_____ _____ within 72 hours of this notice.

If the total of sums due are not paid within 72 hours, please be advised that we will take all legal steps to evict you from the premises.

    I may be reached at _____.

EVICTION NOTICE WORKSHEET
Prepared on: April 28, 2002

Landlord or Manager Name: _____

Address _____

City/State/Zip _____, ___ _____

Rental Unit
Address: _____

City/State/Zip _____, ___ _____

Tenant Name: _____

Social Security No.: _____

Current Address: _____

City/State/Zip _____, ___ _____ Telephone: _____ ext: _____

Reason(s) for Eviction:
Non-payment of rent

76

Rental payment was due on: _____

Rent is delinquent for the month of : _____

    Sincerely,

    Carolyn M. Rosenthal Landlord

Notice of Non-Renewal of Rent

Please consider this to be notice to vacate the premises in 30 days. We do not intend to renew our rental agreement with you.

Thank you for adhering to this request. I may be reached at
_____

    Sincerely,

    Caryl Rosenthal

EVICTION NOTICE WORKSHEET
Prepared on: April 28, 2002

Landlord or Manager Name: _____

Address _____

City/State/Zip _____, ___ _____

Rental Unit
Address: _____

City/State/Zip _____, ___ _____

Tenant Name: _____

Social Security No.: _____

Current Address: _____

City/State/Zip _____, ___ _____ Telephone: _____ ext: _____

Reason(s) for Eviction:

Non-payment of rent
Rental payment was due on: _____

Rent is delinquent for the month of : _____

Amount of monthly rental payment is: $_____

Total amount still due: $_____

The tenant was sent notice of non-payment of rent on _____ _____.
A copy of the letter is attached. Payment must be made by
_____ to avoid possible legal action.

Tenant held over in rental unit after the lease ended
Tenant has been in the rental property for _____ days after the lease period ended.

Violation of rental agreement
Explanation of violation: _____

Illegal activities

Explanation of illegal activities: _____

_____

The following documents regarding the eviction are in the possession of the landlord or manager:

    Letters

    Receipts

    Estimate for repairs

    Canceled check

The following have information which might be useful to support the eviction:

Witness Name: _____ Current Address:

_____

City/State/Zip: _____, ___ _____

Telephone: _____ Ext: _____ Witness knowledge:

_____

Witness Name: _____

Current Address: _____

City/State/Zip: _____, ___ _____

Telephone: _____ Ext: _____ Witness knowledge:

_____

Amount of damage to the rental unit caused by the Tenant: $_____

Description of the damages: _____

There are printed rules governing the rental agreement. A copy of these rules is attached.

The lease is governed by Texas law.

The notice of eviction should be served on the tenant by: the Sheriff.

Possible Tenant defenses to the eviction:

_____

Tenant's Attorney, if known: _____

Address: _____

City/State/Zip: _____, ___ _____

Telephone: _____ ext. _____ Fax Number: _____

Tenant's Employer: _____

Address: _____

City/State/Zip: _____, ___ _____ Telephone: _____ ext. _____

Tenant may contact the landlord or manager by mail at the address given above. Landlord or manager may be contacted by phone at _____, ext._____ .A fax may be sent to _____ .

www.ingramcontent.com/pod-product-compliance
Lightning Source LLC
Chambersburg PA
CBHW060410190526
45169CB00002B/838